Without Spot or Wrinkle

Without Spot or Wrinkle

Reflecting Theologically on the Nature of the Church

Karl Koop and
Mary H. Schertz, editors

WIPF & STOCK · Eugene, Oregon

Wipf and Stock Publishers
199 W 8th Ave, Suite 3
Eugene, OR 97401

Without Spot or Wrinkle
Reflecting Theologically on the Nature of the Church
By Koop, Karl and Schertz, Mary H.
Copyright©2000 Publisher
ISBN 13: 978-1-4982-5056-8
Publication date 5/15/2015
Previously published by Institute of Mennonite Studies, 2000

Contents

Foreword
    J. Nelson Kraybill   1

Introduction
    Karl Koop and Mary Schertz   3

1. *The Church "Without Spot or Wrinkle" in Anabaptist Experience*
    John D. Roth   7

2. *Historical Contexts for MC–GC Integration: Franconia Conference Split (1847) and Russian Migration (1874)*
    James Juhnke   26

3. *Marks of the Church in Galatians: Inheriting a Map without Territory*
    Jo-Ann Brant   38

4. *Faithfulness and Unity in Romans*
    Jacob W. Elias   48

5. *Sola Scriptura/No Other Foundation and Other Authoritative Sources?*
    Ben C. Ollenburger   65

6. *Mennonites and the Church Universal: A Critical Engagement with Miroslav Volf*
    A. James Reimer   93

7. *Polities That Unite and Divide: Magnets and Fences*
    Lois Barrett   112

8. *The Church: Missional Community of the Kingdom*
    John Driver   121

Contributors   137

Foreword

A catalog of popular travel clothing features garments that are "easy care" and "wrinkle-free," that "bend and stretch when you do." Sometimes I wish for a church that would have the same attributes—a church "without a spot or wrinkle or anything of the kind," in the words of Eph. 5:27.

The church may bend and stretch, but it surely is not easy care or wrinkle-free. We Anabaptists—because of persecution or opportunity—have done our share of traveling, but we're still searching for clothes that will remain perfect. Essays in this book display the hopes of Mennonite sojourners who want to lead holy lives and who want the church to reflect the glory of God. The essays also reveal that Mennonites have differing ideas of what constitutes a spot or a wrinkle, and diverse strategies for how the church should respond.

Perhaps it would encourage us to recognize that the early church, too, was a welter of innovation, diversity, and conflict. Much of the New Testament can be understood as inspired attempts to find a way through theological and ecclesiological disputes. We should not expect that the church, this side of eternity, will ever definitively and permanently resolve debates over boundaries and accountability. We may agree that a trinitarian God is at the center of the church, but we will never agree completely on boundaries, fences, and creedal statements.

We should expect, though, that in each generation God will shape enough critical mass of unity for the church to get on with its primary tasks of worship and mission. Important as theological discourse is to the life of the church, our primary objectives are to live and speak the love of God in Jesus Christ.

We might remind ourselves that even the words in Ephesians about being "without a spot or wrinkle" are set like jewels in bands of love. Paul is talking about love between husband and wife, about Christ loving the church, and about tender care for one another (Eph. 5:25–33). In this spirit of nurture, discussion of spots and wrinkles will be redemptive. Before we press too hard toward perfection on our own strength, though, Paul reminds us that the purity of the church is the work of Christ. It will not come to completion until that day when all creation is renewed.

I thank the Institute of Mennonite Studies for organizing the conference at which these papers were presented. I am grateful to each scholar whose work appears in this volume. They have not ironed out all the wrinkles, but have given us a fresh view of the rich fabric that makes up the church.

J. Nelson Kraybill
President, Associated Mennonite Biblical Seminary

Introduction

On February 5, 2000, the Institute of Mennonite Studies held a conference at Associated Mennonite Biblical Seminary entitled "Without Spot or Wrinkle: Reflecting Theologically on the Nature of the Church." This conference gave attention to ecclesiology, in direct response to challenges that Mennonite church bodies in Canada and the United States have been facing in recent times. As Mennonite churches have worked at issues of unity, they have had to address questions related to biblical authority, hermeneutics, church polity, and discipline. All of these questions, of course, are inextricably connected to the nature of the church, a subject that lies at the root of much of the questioning that is taking place in churches today.

The aim of the conference was to provide a context in which conversation about the nature of the church could take place. It was an opportunity for scholars and church leaders to walk with the church in its quest for Christian faithfulness and unity. The presentations of the conference have now been collected in this volume with the hope that conversation on the nature of the church will continue.

The phrase "without spot or wrinkle" comes from Eph. 5:27, a text addressing relationships between husbands and wives within the Christian household. Historically it has also come to symbolize what Mennonites have sometimes believed about the nature of the church. Anabaptists, and Mennonites who came after them, have often maintained that the true church is a gathering of reborn and spiritually regenerated Christians called to be a community free from moral failure. At present, however, some Mennonites are questioning elements of this conceptual legacy, and, in light of personal failings and hurtful church schisms, are expressing doubts about its practical adequacy and theological tenability. Instead of a church "without spot or wrinkle" that seems preoccupied with boundary issues and church discipline, some are seeking alternative directions that they consider to be more at the heart of the gospel.

The essays that follow do not provide a unified argument. What the authors have in common is concern for the church and commitment to faithfulness. Readers are invited to reflect on the issues and make their own assessments.

In the first chapter of this volume, John D. Roth reminds us that the questions of discipline that vex us today are not new. Church discipline has been a central principle and practice as well as a source of profound disagreement for Mennonites since the sixteenth century. Roth contends that the future identity and health of the Mennonite church will depend on Mennonites affirming the centrality of church discipline as foundational to their ecclesiology. This may entail disagreement, conflict, and mutual recognition of incompatible differences, but Mennonites should not avoid the difficult work of discernment and discipline. Moreover, church divisions are not inherently evil, Roth maintains, for they serve to remind us of the richness of God's work in the world, and point to the fact that no group has a monopoly on God's truth.

In the second chapter, James Juhnke gives attention to the historical context of General Conference Mennonite Church–Mennonite Church distinctions. The difference between these two conferences has often been explained in light of the schism that took place in the Franconia Conference in 1847, or in terms of differences in church polity. Juhnke highlights another possible difference, namely, the dissimilarity between Mennonites who trace their ancestry to the Swiss and South German region of the Anabaptist movement, and those who trace their ancestry to the Dutch and North German region of the movement. Juhnke suggests that understanding between the two bodies would be enhanced if these differences were mutually acknowledged, and if the two groups took time to listen to each other's stories.

The next two chapters address the nature of the church using New Testament materials, particularly Pauline writings. Jo-Ann Brant takes up questions related to the marks and boundaries of the church. In her reading of Paul's letters to the Galatians and Corinthians, the morality of law is seen as a guide for the church, but its role is subordinate to the desires of the Spirit. Restoration of transgressors in the Christian community should be carried out in a spirit of gentleness and embrace.

In his study of the book of Romans, Jacob W. Elias continues the discussion by addressing the question of who is to be included in the Christian community. Elias contends that the book of Romans is not in the first place concerned about how individuals can be saved, but about Christian unity, which is essential for the sake of mission. He notes that while it may be impossible for us to agree on all matters, this should not hinder us from attaining unity. He proposes that Christians today follow the pattern of the book of Romans, which gives primary attention to the "big story" of God's own unity, faithfulness, and concern for inclusivity.

Ben C. Ollenburger's essay takes up the question of the authority of Scripture. Scripture has been a primary source of authority in the Anabaptist–Mennonite tradition, but some Mennonites have felt that recent discussions surrounding the issue of homosexuality have not taken Scripture seriously enough. Ollenburger pleads for a high view of Scripture, and maintains that it ought to be understood kerygmatically; that is, Scripture should be read in such a way that the Christian community takes itself to be addressed by God. In conclusion, Ollenburger addresses the status of recent Mennonite church statements on homosexuality, which he believes may have unwittingly undermined the primary authoritative status of Scripture.

In the next chapter, A. James Reimer critically engages the thought of Miroslav Volf on the subject of free-church ecclesiology. He also draws on the views of sixteenth-century Anabaptist theologian Balthasar Hubmaier, and on New Testament (Pauline) ecclesial models, to propose an ecumenically open ecclesiology that would respect both the plurality and the unity of the global Christian community. In his conclusion, Reimer creatively suggests practical implications of his proposal for confession, church polity, and ethics.

The last essays of the volume pay attention to missional concerns. Lois Barrett examines the question of church polity, noting that the church must deal with issues of unity and diversity in ways that maintain right relationships and draw people into relationship with Christ and the church. Unity, however, is not an end in itself. The church must point beyond itself, its mission being to proclaim and be a sign of the reign of God. The only unity worth striving for is the one that makes this mission possible.

Finally, John Driver takes up the subject of mission, and places it at the center of the church's identity. In his view, Mennonites are in danger of following Christendom in defining the church in static and ontological categories. This leads to a misplaced preoccupation with conserving the purity of the church. Driver prefers to follow the biblical traditions imitated by radical communities in church history. These churches are conceived in dynamic and missional terms, shaped by Jesus' own mission. Here believers' concern is not so much for "holding the line" as for putting their lives on the line for the cause of Christ and the kingdom.

The challenges facing the church today are complex and multifaceted. No single volume can address all the issues; neither can it provide definitive answers to the questions that it presumes to address. Nevertheless, as editors, we hope the present volume will contribute to the discussion about the nature of the church and provide direction for Christians as they seek to be faithful to the gospel of Jesus Christ.

We thank the authors for their contributions to this volume. We also thank Barbara Nelson Gingerich, administrative assistant at the Institute of Mennonite Studies, for her careful copy-editing, so this volume could be issued in its present form.

Karl Koop and Mary Schertz

1

The Church "Without Spot or Wrinkle" in Anabaptist Experience

John D. Roth

SETTING A CONTEXT

In the summer of 1660, leaders of various Mennonite churches in the Netherlands met in Leiden to discuss a controversy over the nature of the church that had been sparked by two young ministers from Amsterdam. Several years earlier, Galenus Abrahamsz de Haan and David Spruyt had presented a statement to their co-ministers denying that any church could claim to be the true church of God. Moreover, they argued vigorously that no one's conscience could be bound by the authority of a church office (whose bearers were fallible human beings), or by doctrines formulated by humans, or by ordinances which are always administered by humans.[1] The conference that had convened to address the matter, led by Thielemann Jansz von Braght (whose famous compilation of martyr stories was published that same year), resolved that de Haan and Spruyt should retract these claims or be removed from their ministries.

The men refused to do either. In the decade that followed, the rift separating the two sides found expression in a bitter public exchange of polemical tracts that onlookers from the Reformed Church derisively labeled "The War of the Lambs." Throughout the debate, and to the end of his life, de Haan insisted that unity in the church could be grounded only on the unity of the Spirit, not on some formal confession of faith or fixed list of moral principles. And, from the broad perspective of Dutch Mennonite history, his was the voice that eventually prevailed. In the

---

[1] For a full recounting of the events, see S. Blaupot ten Cate, *Geschiedenis der Doopsgezinden in Holland, Zeeland, Utrecht en Gelderland* I (Amsterdam: P. N. van Kampen, 1847). Unfortunately, the full details of this story are scarcely known to an English-speaking audience. The most accessible account I could find is in H. W. Meihuizen, "Spiritualistic Tendencies and Movements among the Dutch Mennonites of the 16th and 17th Centuries," *Mennonite Quarterly Review* 27 (October 1953): 288–91.

aftermath of the dispute, a series of congregational mergers took place—Haarlem (1672), Koog-Zaandijk (1680), Alkmaar (1692), Rotterdam (1700), and Leyden (1701)—all of which drew explicitly on the logic and spirit of de Haan's extensive writings. When all of the various branches of Dutch Mennonitism were formally united into a single church a century later, the basis of the union was not a statement of shared doctrines or a list of ordinances. Instead the groups came together around a general appeal to the unity of the Spirit and the explicit assurance that "every congregation kept its freedom to make such decisions about doctrine as it wished, without the right to bind others to their convictions."[2]

Just as the War of the Lambs was coming to an end in the Netherlands, another controversy was brewing among the Swiss Brethren, spiritual cousins of the Dutch Mennonites living in the Jura highlands of Switzerland and on scattered estates in the Alsace and the Palatinate.[3] In many respects, the Swiss Brethren differed sharply from their Dutch counterparts. Whereas the Dutch were largely urban, wealthy, highly-educated, and skilled in the arts of rhetorical exchange, the Swiss Brethren were an agrarian people, led by an unschooled, unpaid lay ministry, living at the margins of Swiss society under the persistent cloud of civil and physical persecution. But despite these differences, the debate that tore through their community in the 1690s bore some striking similarities to the key issues in the War of the Lambs.

In the late summer of 1693, Swiss Brethren congregations in Alsace—congregations established by refugees who had been forced to flee Switzerland—commissioned Jakob Ammann and several other ministers to make an investigative journey to the Emmental. These ministers were to clarify the mother church's position on questions regarding the nature of the church, particularly issues related to the practice of church discipline. From the outset, conversations between Ammann and Hans Reist, the senior minister in the Emmental region, were filled with tension. Ammann rebuked the Swiss congregations for ignoring open sin in their midst, and claimed that the Swiss had ceased to uphold church discipline as established by Christ in Matthew 18. Ammann's group was also troubled because Reist and his ministers taught that their non-Anabaptist neighbors—who had not been baptized

---

[2] Quoted in Meihuizen, "Spiritualist Tendencies," 303.

[3] The story of the Amish division is told in a succinct way by Steven M. Nolt in *A History of the Amish* (Intercourse, Pa.: Good Books, 1992), 23–41.

and who were outside the fellowship of a covenanted community—might nonetheless be saved. Reist responded by challenging Ammann's authority to bring such charges and by insisting that Christ looks on the heart, not on external matters.

Like the War of the Lambs, the subsequent exchange was passionate and acrimonious. In the end, despite several efforts at reunification, the Swiss Brethren church remained divided. Over the past three centuries, the Amish and the Mennonite heirs to this conflict have continued to claim the same biblically-based Anabaptist heritage, and each has preserved some notion of the visible church and the practice of church discipline. Yet the central issues that divided Ammann and Reist have not disappeared and the two groups remain clearly divided to this day.

I offer these two vignettes from the late seventeenth century, not because they are somehow paradigmatic of the entire historical Anabaptist-Mennonite understanding of the church, but because they remind us that the issues of church polity, theology, ethics, and ecclesiology that vex us today are deeply rooted in our past. They also remind us that the resolution of these conflicts has pointed in sharply different—even contradictory—directions. I also want to call to our attention the fact that our decisions about these matters have real historical consequences. A hundred years from now, historians will look back on the series of decisions made at the turn of the twentieth century and will make judgments about the wisdom of those decisions in light of the consequences that emerged from them.

With these stories in mind, consider the following general theses that I think reflect the essence of the Anabaptist-Mennonite understanding of the church "without spot or wrinkle."

CHURCH DISCIPLINE AS A CENTRAL THEME IN THE ANABAPTIST-MENNONITE TRADITION

Thesis 1: The principle and practice of church discipline has been foundational to a distinctively Anabaptist-Mennonite understanding of the church.

From a historical perspective, teachings on church discipline cannot be ignored or minimized without substantively altering the core of Anabaptist-Mennonite understandings of faithfulness. The centrality of church discipline modeled after the pattern laid out by Christ in Matthew 18 was evident from the very origins of the Anabaptist movement. Already in September 1524, at least six months before the first adult baptisms in Zurich and the formal beginnings of a voluntary church, Conrad Grebel admonished another radical reformer, Thomas Müntzer, to "create a Christian church with the help of Christ and His rule as we find it instituted in Matthew 18 and practiced in the epistles." Then, articulating the basic principles that would appear repeatedly in the writings of other Anabaptists, Grebel instructed Müntzer to "apply it with earnestness and common prayer and restraint, in line with faith and love, and without law and compulsion."[4]

After the emergence of separatist congregations in Zurich and the outlying areas, the principle of church discipline quickly became one of the distinguishing features of the nascent Anabaptist movement. Balthasar Hubmaier, the most gifted theologian of the early Swiss Brethren, included references to Matthew 18 in virtually all of his writings, and he devoted two tracts exclusively to the subject.[5] In 1527, when internal dissension threatened to destroy the movement, Anabaptists gathered secretly at the small village of Schleitheim in a conscious effort to restore unity on the basis of Matthew 18. The second article of the "Brotherly Union" established at that gathering explicitly affirmed their commitment to the practice of church discipline and the ban. In the course of the following decades, Swiss Brethren leaders referred to Matthew 18, "the rule of Christ," "binding and loosing" or the ban as a central feature of their theology in virtually every printed tract, treatise, or public disputation that addressed issues related to the church.[6]

---

[4] Quoted in Leland Harder, ed., *The Sources of Swiss Anabaptism*, Classics of the Radical Reformation, vol. 4 (Scottdale, Pa., and Kitchener, Ont.: Herald Press, 1985), 289-90.

[5] See his "On Fraternal Admonition," and "On the Christian Ban," in H. Wayne Pipkin and John H. Yoder, trans. and eds., *Balthasar Hubmaier: Theologian of Anabaptism*, Classics of the Radical Reformation, vol. 5 (Scottdale, Pa., and Kitchener, Ont.: Herald Press, 1989), 372-85 and 409-25.

[6] The issue emerges, for example, in the public disputation with Pfistermeyer (1531), at Zofingen (1532) and at Bern (1538), and again at Frankenthal (1571). The Scripture index in Martin Haas, ed., *Drei Täufergespräche*, Quellen zur Geschichte der Täufer in der Schweiz, vol. 4 (Zurich: Theologischer Verlag, 1974), 485, lists dozens of references to Matthew 18. See also the unpublished manuscript by Thomas Meyer, "Vonn dem Christen[lichen] Bann" [1575], Staatsarchiv Zurich [Arnold Snyder has made a transcription of this document, a copy of which is located in The Mennonite Historical Library, Goshen College, Goshen, Ind.]. Ervin A. Schlabach, "The Rule of Christ among the Early Swiss

The concern for church discipline was not merely theoretical. References to Anabaptist standards of moral purity—particularly the contrast in ethical behavior between Swiss Brethren and members of the state churches—recur repeatedly throughout court records, interrogation protocol, and the correspondence preserved in the *Täuferakten*.[7]

Nor was this principle an eccentricity of the South German–Swiss Brethren wing of the Anabaptist movement. The theme permeates the voluminous writings of Menno Simons, who struggled to bring theological clarity and cohesion to the Dutch Anabaptist movement in the aftermath of the debacle at Münster.[8] Dirk Philips, whose writings stood alongside Menno's as the anchor of the North German–Dutch Anabaptist theological tradition, wrote extensively on the subject.[9] The biblical practice of church discipline was also at the core of Hutterite teachings on community of goods;[10] it emerged as a central theme in the

---

Anabaptists" (Ph.D. diss., Chicago Theological Seminary, 1977) provides the best general overview of the Swiss Brethren understanding of church discipline.

[7] See, for example, John C. Wenger, "Martin Weninger's Vindication of Anabaptism, 1535" *Mennonite Quarterly Review* 22 (July 1948), 180–87, which criticizes the state church for tolerating all manner of sin. They "consider the gospel a burden which no one can keep" and, lacking the ban, they care not at all "whether a person does evil or good" (185).

[8] Menno wrote extensively on the subject of church discipline and the ban. See the following treatises published in Leonard Verduin, trans., and J. C. Wenger, ed., *The Complete Writings of Menno Simons* (Scottdale, Pa.: Herald Press, 1956): "A Kind Admonition on Church Discipline" (1541), 407–18; "A Clear Account of Excommunication" (1550), 457–76; "Instruction on Discipline to the Church at Franeker" (1555), 1043–45; "Instruction on Discipline to the Church at Emden" (1556), 1050–51; "Instruction on Excommunication" (1558), 959–98; and "Reply to Sylis and Lemke" (1560), 1000–1015.

[9] For a good summary of Dirk's understanding of discipline and the ban, see his article on "The Ban" from his *Enchiridion*, and the essay "Evangelical Excommunication" [1567], in C. J. Dyck, William Keeney, and Alvin Beachy, trans. and ed., *The Writings of Dirk Philips, 1504–1568*, Classics of the Radical Reformation, vol. 6 (Scottdale, Pa., and Waterloo, Ont.: Herald Press, 1992), 238–54 and 591–610. Philips also likely wrote "A Confession About Separation" (611–17) and may have been the author of "Omitted Writing about the Ban and Avoidance," (578–88).

[10] See John J. Friesen, trans. and ed., *Peter Riedemann's Hutterite Confession of Faith*, Classics of the Radical Reformation, vol. 9 (Waterloo, Ont., and Scottdale, Pa.: Herald Press, 1999), 152–53.

Amish tradition;[11] it continued to shape the religious worldview of the Mennonite groups that emigrated to the Russian Empire in the nineteenth century;[12] and it persisted as a central concern within the Mennonite settlements and congregations in the U.S. and Canadian diaspora.[13] A perusal of Howard Loewen's compilation of Mennonite confessions of faith makes it clear that virtually every doctrinal statement in the Dutch, Prussian, Russian, Swiss, or South German Mennonite tradition includes some reference to church discipline as an essential feature of the New Testament church.[14]

To be sure, the historical contexts of these various references differed widely, and among the numerous authors who addressed the theme, one can discern important nuances in exegesis and emphasis. Seen as a whole, however, a set of consistently recurring arguments and understandings do emerge out of this large body of materials.

1. The practice of church discipline is biblical. In public defenses and in private admonitions, Anabaptist leaders repeatedly appealed to Scripture to explain and to justify the importance of church discipline in

---

[11] See the documents collected in John D. Roth, trans. and ed., *Letters of the Amish Division: A Sourcebook* (Goshen, Ind.: Mennonite Historical Society, 1993), esp. 53–77, 83–110; and Brad Igou, comp., *The Amish in Their Own Words: Amish Writings from 25 Years of Family Life Magazine* (Scottdale, Pa.: Herald Press, 1999), 207–30, offers an accessible window into the contemporary Amish understanding of discipline and the ban.

[12] See James Urry, *None But Saints: The Transformation of Mennonite Life in Russia, 1789–1889* (Winnipeg: Hyperion Press, 1989), esp. 174–95. Jacob A. Loewen and Wesley J. Prieb, *Only the Sword of the Spirit* (Winnipeg: Kindred Productions, 1997), offer many examples of what they see as abuses of power in the Russian Mennonite tradition.

[13] See the 4-volume The Mennonite Experience in America Series, esp. vol. 2, by Theron F. Schlabach, *Peace, Faith, Nation: Mennonites and Amish in Nineteenth-Century America* (Scottdale, Pa., and Kitchener, Ont.: Herald Press, 1988), with its numerous references to discipline, church, the ban, and shunning as part of the self-differentiation that took place among Mennonites and Amish during the nineteenth century.

[14] Howard John Loewen, *One Lord, One Church, One Hope, and One God: Mennonite Confessions of Faith*, Text Reader Series, no. 2 (Elkhart, Ind.: Institute of Mennonite Studies, 1985); see esp. the summary and tables on 260–67.

their doctrine and practice.[15] The cornerstone text was the teaching of Christ in Matthew 18, which offered both a mandate and a procedure for discipline. Almost as frequently, one finds references to the Pauline texts of 1 Corinthians 12 (especially verses 25-27, admonishing the body to unity) or 2 Corinthians 6 (verses 14-18, which stress the separated nature of the faithful church from the fallen world). Although Anabaptist writers only rarely cited Eph. 5:27—the passage concerning the church "without spot or wrinkle"—their defense of the principle was consistently rooted in Scripture.

2. *The exercise of church discipline was not to be punitive, but rather was intended as an expression of love for the erring member or group.* In the apologetic writings of theologians such as Hubmaier, Marpeck, Menno, and Riedemann, as well as in the numerous Anabaptist-Mennonite confessions of faith that emerged later, discussions of discipline or the ban repeatedly begin with a clear statement that the intent of church discipline is to restore a wayward member to a fuller understanding of faith, discipleship, and relations within the fellowship of believers.[16] Though one can find examples where this ideal was flagrantly violated, the stated goal of church discipline has consistently been the spiritual health and well-being of the offender.

3. *Church discipline is an essential corollary to the Anabaptist principles of voluntary baptism and pacifism.* The Anabaptists rejected infant baptism, insisting that membership in the congregation was the result of a voluntary choice. The individual joined the group freely, knowing in advance the doctrines and standards *(Ordnung)* of the group. Therefore, the integrity of both the voluntary choice and the moral character of the congregation could be preserved only if the community exercised discipline in relation to members whose beliefs or actions later proved to be at odds with those of the congregation. Otherwise, as

---

[15] See, for example, the *Concordantz und Zeiger der namhafftigsten Sprüch aller biblischen Bücher*, one of the earliest known concordances among the Anabaptists, where reference to discipline appears under a wide variety of headings such as "love," "separation [from the world]," and "sin," as well as in the section on "brotherly discipline." The concordance, first published in the 1530s or 1540s by the Swiss Brethren, was reprinted in several Dutch editions and also in German in the seventeenth and eighteenth century.

[16] This is clearly the primary point of Thomas Meyer's treatment of the ban (see footnote 6 above).

Anabaptists never tired of pointing out, the baptismal choice was meaningless.[17] A church without discipline might just as well baptize babies since, to their way of thinking, moral or theological standards are ultimately meaningless in such a congregation. Discipline guaranteed that the voluntary decision to become a member of the church remained ongoing (i.e., that membership continued to be an active choice).

In a related fashion, discipline practiced in accordance with Matthew 18 was also a clear testimony to the nonviolent rule of Christ. In sharp contrast to the state churches, whose unity was preserved by the coercive practices of intimidation, torture, and executions, the Anabaptists insisted that the conscience could not be swayed by physical force.[18] The biblical model of the ban and shunning was consistent with Christ's teaching of nonviolent active love.

4. Church discipline underscored the Anabaptist conviction that no one could truly know Christ, unless he followed after Christ in life.[19] Repeatedly, Anabaptist spokespersons insisted that a church that did not expect moral regeneration in the life of the believer made a mockery of the power of the incarnation and God's saving act in Christ. Although this point stirred up frequent charges of Pelagianism and moral perfectionism, the Anabaptists argued that claiming the experience of grace and debating about Christian doctrines were both empty exercises if they were not linked to a life of daily Christian discipleship. Discipline thus underscored the efficacy of Christ's salvific power and of the Spirit's enabling grace to transform the moral character of believers.

5. Finally, church discipline was an essential part of the Anabaptist-Mennonite view of mission, especially the corporate witness of the church. In their understanding, the integrity of the church's mission to a fallen world rested on the church's own unity in matters of faith and practice. Few Anabaptists actually argued that the church could somehow be perfect, "without spot or wrinkle." But healthy congregations sought constantly to mold themselves into the image of

---

[17] For only one example of this, see the argument developed by Balthasar Hubmaier in "A Christian Catechism," in Pipkin and Yoder, eds., *Balthasar Hubmaier*, 349-54.

[18] See *Balthasar Hubmaier*, 351; for Hubmaier's insistence on the link between baptism and fraternal admonition, see 381, 384, 389, 416.

[19] See Hans Denck, "The Contention that Scripture Says," in *Anabaptism in Outline: Selected Primary Sources,* ed. Walter Klaassen (Kitchener, Ont., and Scottdale, Pa.: Herald Press, 1981), 87.

Christ. And without the practice of discipline, the church as a gathered body of believers would cease to be visible to its neighbors.[20]

In summary, the teaching and practice of church discipline has been a central tenet of the Anabaptist-Mennonite tradition for virtually all groups and for most of our 475-year history. Far from being an eccentric obsession of a few conservative groups, the goal of a disciplined, visible church has been at the heart of our self-understanding. Indeed, those groups that rejected the practice of church discipline, or allowed it to atrophy, almost inevitably lost their distinctive identity, declined in numbers, and became assimilated into other denominations or into the broader culture. To stand within the Anabaptist-Mennonite tradition virtually demands that one engage the question of church discipline.

CHURCH DISCIPLINE AS A LOCUS OF CONFLICT
IN THE ANABAPTIST-MENNONITE TRADITION

Thesis 2: For virtually all of our 475-year history, the teachings and practices regarding church discipline have been a source of profound disagreements, intense conflicts, and numerous schisms within the Anabaptist-Mennonite church.

While church discipline has indeed been a central theme in Anabaptist-Mennonite theology, few issues have been more contentious in actual practice than the elusive ideal of the church "without spot or wrinkle."

In part, controversies associated with church discipline were simply an inevitable corollary of its practice. After all, discipline only becomes relevant when believers find themselves at odds with each other on matters of faith or practice. But the Anabaptists' egalitarian bias in their approach to reading and interpreting scripture, their insistence that faith

---

[20] See Franklin H. Littell, "What Butzer Debated with the Anabaptists at Marburg: A Document of 1538," *Mennonite Quarterly Review* 36 (July 1962): 256–76. Pilgrim Marpeck, who constantly sought a via media between what he perceived to be the excessive legalism of the Swiss Brethren and the individualism of the spiritualists, makes this point explicitly in "The Admonition of 1542," in William Klassen and Walter Klaassen, trans. and ed., *The Writings of Pilgrim Marpeck*, Classics of the Radical Reformation, vol. 2 (Scottdale, Pa., and Kitchener, Ont.: Herald Press, 1978), 295–97. Ernst Müller, *Geschichte der bernischen Täufer* (Frauenfeld: I. Huber, 1895), 107–31, provides numerous testimonies from interrogations in which the appeal of the Anabaptists in the canton of Bern during the seventeenth century was clearly linked to the seriousness with which the Anabaptists practiced church discipline.

must bear fruit in daily life, and their concern that the gathered body of believers be united in faith and practice meant that differing understandings of the Bible could often be resolved only by appealing to the principles of Matthew 18.

Each of the many conflicts sparked by the debate over discipline had its own unique context in which personality clashes, high-minded appeals to principle, exegetical differences, political pressures, and economic considerations all found expression. Nevertheless, the debates frequently played themselves out along predictable lines.

1. Church discipline within the Anabaptist-Mennonite tradition tended to focus on ethical and cultural issues rather than on doctrinal matters. To be sure, Mennonites debated mightily over Scripture and often found themselves deeply divided over how it should be interpreted. But the practice of church discipline—and the divisions that sometimes ensued—hinged much more frequently on debates over ethical matters (especially issues related to truth-telling, marriage commitments, sexuality, nonresistance) or on disagreements about cultural practices that defined the boundary between the visible church and the fallen world. Examples from the latter category are legion, relating to such issues as dress regulations, symbols of modernity, transportation and communication technology, honoring the Sabbath, etc. At the heart of these controversies was the ancient challenge of separating essential features of Christian life and practice—those principles whose integrity required the practice of church discipline—from things adiaphora—matters about which Christians of goodwill could agree to disagree.

2. Another focus of conflict within the Anabaptist-Mennonite tradition related to the manner in which church discipline should be exercised, especially in regards to its severity. According to Matthew 18, the final step in the disciplinary process was to treat the erring member as "a tax collector and a sinner." But what this meant in the context of early modern Europe was not always clear. Already within the first half-century of the Anabaptist movement, a kind of graded scale of severity had emerged which served to distinguish some groups from others. Among some groups, church discipline meant that the disciplined member could no longer take communion but could participate in congregational life in every other respect (*kleine Bann*). Other groups formally dropped the disciplined individual from the church membership roll and rejected any further involvement of the former member in the life of the congregation (*große Bann*). Still others insisted that the ban and the rule of Christ required that the congregation formally impose a pattern of social avoidance (*Meidung*) on the wayward individual or group, which forbade any economic and social interactions with those who had been disciplined.[21] When matters were pushed to the extreme, as for example in the debate between Dutch and German Mennonites in the 1570s, the shunning of an excommunicated member extended into the family, even to the point of forbidding members of the church to sleep with their excommunicated spouses (marital avoidance).[22]

3. *Anabaptist-Mennonite groups frequently differed with each other in their understandings of where the authority to initiate and carry out church discipline was ultimately lodged.* Was the exercise of church discipline something that the entire congregation had to affirm, or could individual pastors or influential bishops serve as both judge and jury in matters of discipline? Did the locus of decision-making in matters of faith and practice rest, as seemed to be the case with Menno Simons and Dirk Philips, primarily with the elders in informal consultation with each other? Or did it reside in formal documents that were generated at regional conferences by representatives from local congregations? Or did the local congregation function independently of other congregations or conferences? Only in the Dutch tradition, following the union of 1811, did a radically congregational polity find explicit affirmation. Much more common in the Anabaptist-Mennonite tradition were efforts to forge regional unity through the creation of shared confessions of faith[23] or through the so-called disciplines or ordinances summarized at

---

[21] For a good review of these nuances, see Harold S. Bender, "Excommunication, Procedure and Grounds," in *The Mennonite Encyclopedia* (Scottdale, Pa.: Mennonite Publishing House; Newton, Kans.: Mennonite Publication Office; Hillsboro, Kans.: Mennonite Brethren Publishing House, 1956), 2:277-79.

[22] See the account of this debate in Cornelius Krahn, *Dutch Anabaptism: Origin, Spread, Life, and Thought (1450-1600)* (The Hague: Martinus Nijhoff, 1968), 229-37. For a modern version of this contentious issue that has gained notoriety in the secular press, see Robert L. Bear, *Delivered unto Satan* (Carlisle, Pa.: Bear, 1974).

[23] This is clearly the turn taken by the Dutch in the seventeenth and eighteenth centuries, as detailed in Karl Koop's recent dissertation, "Early Seventeenth-Century Mennonite Confessions of Faith: The Development of an Anabaptist Tradition" (PhD. diss., U. of St. Michael's College and the Toronto School of Theology, 1999).

conferences, which were understood to be binding on all the congregations who had been present at the meeting.[24]

4. *Finally, from the beginning of the Anabaptist movement, church discipline and the practice of the ban were applied to groups as well as to individuals.* Unlike their Catholic and Protestant neighbors, the Anabaptists did not have an episcopal hierarchy or a formal systematic theology to adjudicate conflicting interpretations of Scripture. In the absence of these authorities, the exercise of church discipline became an important means of defining group identity.

The use of church discipline as a means of sharpening group identity began early. The Schleitheim confession of 1527, after all, emerged as a means of clarifying the boundaries that separated those who affirmed its seven articles from the "false brethren," fellow reformers who were presumably misleading new believers. In his book *Hutterite Beginnings*, historian Werner Packull painstakingly details the acrimonious beginnings of the Hutterites in the 1530s and 1540s, a story filled with the frequent and mutual application of the ban by leaders upon each other and their respective groups.[25] In January 1531, veteran Swiss Brethren missionary Wilhelm Reublin, who had been sojourning among Anabaptist groups in Moravia, reported to his co-worker Pilgrim Marpeck that he had been "badly deceived" about the brotherhood in Austerlitz, where the elders were "false deceivers, untrue in doctrine, life

---

[24] This is present in the Dutch tradition (e.g. Wismar, Cologne), but probably more prevalent among the Swiss–South Germans beginning with a series of gatherings in Strasbourg in the 1550s. See Harold S. Bender, "The Discipline Adopted by the Strasbourg Conference of 1568," *Mennonite Quarterly Review* 1 (January 1927): 57–66; and John S. Oyer, "The Strasbourg Conferences of the Anabaptists, 1554–1607," *Mennonite Quarterly Review* 58 (July 1984): 218–29. For a helpful summary of the longer trajectory of ordinances compiled at these and later conferences, see William R. McGrath, *Christian Discipline: How and Why the Anabaptists Made Church Standards* (Carrollton, Ohio: Amish Mennonite Publications, 1989).

[25] See especially Werner O. Packull, "Dissension in the 'Congregation of God': The Schisms of 1531 and 1533," in *Hutterite Beginnings: Communitarian Experiments during the Reformation* (Baltimore: Johns Hopkins Univ. Press, 1995), 214–35. See also Packull's treatment of the use of the ban among the early Hutterites, in *Rereading Anabaptist Beginnings* (Winnipeg: Canadian Mennonite Bible College, 1991), 59–78.

and work in each and every point."²⁶ By mid-century, relations between the Hutterites and the Swiss Brethren had become frankly hostile. In 1557, when a large number of Swiss Brethren near Kreuznach left their congregation to join the Hutterites in Moravia, the congregation's leader—a man named Farwendel—called the Hutterites a "cursed people" and excommunicated himself for not having guarded his flock sufficiently against the Hutterites.²⁷ By the 1560s, the two groups had effectively banned each other.

Better known, perhaps, is the story of conflict between the Dutch Anabaptists and the Swiss Brethren, which culminated in 1560 when Menno and the Dutch elders pronounced the ban on the Swiss and German congregations for being lax in the practice of discipline, particularly in regards to marital shunning. Only a few years later, the Dutch church itself was divided when the so-called Waterlanders broke with Menno and other leaders over the issue of the ban, a division that was followed in 1567 by yet another major split within the Dutch church, between the Frisians and the Flemish. So acrimonious was the Frisian/Flemish division that when the Zierikezee congregation attempted to retain a judicious neutrality in the debate, it found itself excommunicated by both parties.²⁸ The flurry of excommunications that rocked Dutch Anabaptism in the 1560s and 1570s reached a point of diminishing returns in the instance of Jan van Ophoorn, a Flemish pastor at Emden, who established a church in his own house with only himself and his wife as member.²⁹

---

²⁶ John C. Wenger, trans. and ed., "A Letter from Wilhelm Reublin to Pilgram Marpeck, 1531," *Mennonite Quarterly Review* 23 (April 1949): 69.

²⁷ The story comes from Claus Peter Clasen, *Anabaptism: A Social History: 1525-1618: Switzerland, Austria, Moravia, South and Central Germany* (Ithaca: Cornell Univ. Press, 1972), 40. This is apparently not the complete story, however, since Farwendel ended up joining the Hutterites. See Leonard Gross, *The Golden Years of the Hutterites: The Witness and Thought of the Communal Moravian Anabaptists during the Walpot Era, 1565-1578* (Scottdale, Pa.: Herald Press, 1980), 166; *The Chronicle of the Hutterian Brethren* (Rifton, N.Y.: Plough, 1987), 1:331.

²⁸ Christian Neff, "Flemish Mennonites," *Mennonite Encyclopedia,* 2:238.

²⁹ Van der Zijpp, "Jan (Hans) van Ophoorn," *Mennonite Encyclopedia,* 3:79-80. In the midst of these internal conflicts, played out against the backdrop of persecution and martyrdom, Dutch Anabaptist Job Jost penned a prayer that included the following: "O God, give me grace that I may be delivered from this

The litany of other schisms, solidified by the exercise of church discipline, is a long one indeed. A full telling of that story would need to include a more complete account of Amish beginnings, the emergence of the Collegiants in Netherlands and the Dompelaars in West Prussia, the 1810 origins of the Kleine Gemeinde church among the Mennonite immigrants to Russia, and, a half century later, the establishment of the Mennonite Brethren in the same region. In North America, the story of new churches established in the midst of conflict by John Oberholtzer, Daniel Brenneman, and Henry Egli is only a small part of the complex and fascinating account of Mennonite self-differentiation in North America during the past 300 years.[30]

In all of these conflicts, debates over the principle and practice of church discipline run like an iron thread throughout our 475-year history. The Anabaptist-Mennonites' high view of Christ as moral exemplar, along with their commitment to the principle of voluntary baptism and the witness of the visible church meant that how believers expressed their faith in daily life mattered enough to argue about it. And that process of discernment could—and frequently did—lead to conflicts and schisms.

OUR CHALLENGE: TO EMBRACE BOTH DISCIPLINE AND CONFLICT

The historical trajectory of the Anabaptist-Mennonite tradition sketched above leaves us with an ambiguous picture of the understanding and practice of church discipline. On the one hand, the principle has been an essential feature of our theological and ecclesiastical self-understanding. Yet few issues have been as consistently vexing or conflict-ridden as church discipline. Where does this leave us? In my final thesis I will take the risky step of moving from the past to the present, to offer my own reading on the potential relevance of our history for the church today as we struggle to sort out the meaning of church discipline for our own day.

---

wicked fury and may live for half a year in a quiet and peaceful place; then shall I gladly offer up my body for the faith." Quoted in Anna Brons, *Ursprung, Entwickelung und Schicksale der Taufgesinnten oder Mennoniten* (Norden: Diedr. Soltau, 1884), 136–37.

[30] See, for example, the fascinating overview of the various conservative groups in Stephen Scott, *An Introduction to Old Order and Conservative Mennonite Groups* (Intercourse, Pa.: Good Books, 1996), which includes references to groups containing fewer than a dozen members.

Thesis 3: The future identity and health of the Mennonite church will depend on our willingness to boldly embrace both Thesis 1 and Thesis 2.

A healthy Mennonite church of the future will continue to affirm the centrality of church discipline as foundational to our ecclesiology and our understanding of Christian faithfulness. And it will do so knowing that a commitment to the hard work of discernment necessarily entails disagreements, conflicts, and maybe even the mutual recognition of incompatible differences.

The temptation to avoid the hard work of discernment, to dodge the pain of conflict, to jettison the principle and practice of church discipline, and to allow the Matthew 18 text to fade quietly into the museum of the Mennonite past is extremely powerful. Pressures to do precisely this come from at least three sources that I would like to acknowledge, and challenge.

One voice calling for the elimination of church discipline comes from within the Anabaptist-Mennonite tradition itself in the form of a spiritualist dissent that has challenged the very concept of the visible church.[31] Hans Denck was perhaps the first Anabaptist to articulate this position, but it quickly became a recurring theme among other voices at the margin of the Anabaptist movement, including those of Sebastian Franck, Caspar Schwenckfeld, Christian Entfelder, Hans Bünderlin, David Joris, Obbe Philipps, and Abrahamsz Galenus de Haan.

The argument itself has taken varied expressions. Some, like Hans Denck and Christian Entfelder, argued that God's essentially loving, gracious, and forgiving nature made it unthinkable that He—much less mortal human beings—could pronounce words of spiritual judgment on another person. Others, like Caspar Schwenckfeld, rejected all institutions, rituals, and ordinances as human creations that inevitably supplant the Creator as the object of our worship. Later splinter groups—such as the Dutch Collegiants of the seventeenth and eighteenth centuries—argued from a kind of epistemological humility that human beings can never fully know the mind of God. They therefore rejected discipline as presumptuous and arrogant. In later centuries, a variety of

---

[31] Meihuizen, "Spiritualist Tendencies," offers a sympathetic portrayal of the spiritualist trajectory among Dutch Anabaptists. The best general overview of this tension within the broader Anabaptist tradition is found in C. Arnold Snyder, *Anabaptist History and Theology: An Introduction* (Kitchener, Ont.: Pandora Press, 1995), 299–350.

evangelical renewal movements within Mennonite and Amish groups have regarded church discipline as a form of works-righteousness that undermines the saving grace of God whose power cannot be bound by the human will. More recently, appeals to the spiritual authority of psychology and therapeutic counseling have dramatically eroded the exercise of church discipline.

Evidence of these assumptions within the contemporary Mennonite church can be read in the well-practiced impulse of many of my students to quote the passage, "Judge not lest ye be judged," when asked about the moral choices they or their friends are making. Numerous letters to *The Mennonite*, the *Mennonite Weekly Review* or *The Canadian Mennonite* also resolve ethical conundrums not on the basis of scriptural or theological discernment, but by preemptively identifying any congregational or ecclesiastical standard as—by definition—oppressive and legalistic.

At their best, all of these impulses share a conviction that the power of the Spirit cannot be harnessed by human codes, that human forms of authority are as likely to destroy as to build up, that church discipline is a human rather than a divine exercise. But the consequence of this reasoning is a direct challenge to any discernment process that imposes normative standards of faith or practice within the fellowship of believers.

A second impulse to avoid the tensions inherent in the practice of church discipline is associated with larger patterns of change in the religious landscape of North American culture. As religious sociologists have been pointing out for at least a decade, one of the most striking characteristics of modern American religious life is the steady decline of denominational loyalty, especially among mainline Protestant groups.[32] Increasingly, religiously-oriented people in the United States and Canada are embracing a kind of generic Christianity cut free from historical traditions, doctrinal claims, or clearly-defined ethical norms. And they are doing this not out of a passionate affirmation of Christ's prayer for

---

[32] The observation has been made frequently in the literature. For a helpful point of departure see Robert Wuthnow, *The Restructuring of American Religion: Society and Faith since World War II* (Princeton: Princeton Univ. Press, 1988), 88; John P. Dever, "Fading Denominationalism: New Concepts of Church," *Review and Expositor* (Fall 1993), 505–7; and Roger Finke and Rodney Stark, *The Churching of America, 1776–1990: Winners and Losers in Our Religious Economy* (New Brunswick, N.J.: Rutgers Univ. Press, 1992).

unity in John 17, but as an extension of the logic of market capitalism in which Christians are free to shop for the church or congregation that best suits their individual taste or needs. In such a context, the practice of church discipline, in which members agree to hold themselves accountable to certain principles or behaviors, becomes virtually irrelevant.

A third argument for allowing church discipline to atrophy has emerged as a reflexive reaction against the history of conflict that discipline has engendered. This impulse is particularly evident among the current generation of Mennonite leaders who hold memories (often in the form of stories handed down from their parents) of church splits over picayune details. They have heard about the capricious or abusive exercise of power by male bishops or the lingering pain of exclusion that lives on in the family stories of a relative who suffered the consequences of church discipline long ago. In many conversations, the personal and particular memory of church discipline badly exercised can quickly trump the whole sweep of the broader tradition and any theological or principled arguments one might make in defense of Matthew 18. This is not to deny that real abuse has indeed occurred in our past; but replacing bad discipline with no discipline at all is hardly a sensible solution.

Why are these options unacceptable? Why should we continue to wrestle, even painfully, with issues related to church discipline? In addition to all of the reasons offered by the Anabaptists (see Thesis 1), I offer by way of conclusion a few additional arguments.

Spiritualists and "generic Christians," I would argue, are deluding themselves if they think that they can practice a form of Christianity that is freed from all doctrine, norms, or discipline. Christian faith always has an embodied form. Even those who emphasize the primacy of the Spirit express their convictions in words and deeds that have a cultural shape. Would-be generic Christians always bring a hermeneutical grid to their interpretation of Scripture; their Sunday school curriculum reflects a theological tradition; their pastors are trained at someone's seminary. To deny the legitimacy of discipline, even if it is only implicit, is to be blind to the ways in which one's life is indeed shaped by the norms and expectations of others—if not of a body of believers then of the culture at large. In reality, the option today, as in the sixteenth century, is not whether one will have allegiances that are bound by time and space, but only where these allegiances will be focused.

To those who fear the abuse of power inherent in the exercise of church discipline, I offer the observation that the long record of the

Anabaptist-Mennonite tradition testifies to the fact that membership in the gathered body of believers is the beginning of conversation, not the end of it. Voluntary adult baptism does not imply an absolute commitment to a set of fixed beliefs or a rigid code of conduct. Instead baptism signifies a commitment to the difficult, dynamic, and life-giving task of discernment: of reading the cultural context, studying the Scriptures, listening to the voice of the Holy Spirit, and testing one's impulses and assumptions against the wisdom of fellow and sister believers.

In the process of discernment, conflict is inevitable. Conflict is an unavoidable part of figuring out the meaning of faithfulness for each generation and for each setting. It would be tragic if, out of fear that we will end up with the wrong answers (as our foreparents did on occasion), we either refused to enter into the conversation or resorted to a minimalist understanding of God's will that retreats into private truth and ethical pluralism. The conflict inherent in discernment is the means by which we test and reformulate our personal convictions within a larger frame of reference.

Finally, even when discernment is done carefully and with integrity, conflicts can—and sometimes must—lead to the separation of an individual from the larger body, or to the formation of two distinct groups. To foreclose on the possibility of division from the beginning of the conversation, or to insist from the outset that conversations and discernment continue indefinitely, is ultimately to make conversion, discernment, and missions unintelligible. To be sure, much more needs to be said about the process of conversation prior to division, about the need for personal and corporate humility, and about the appropriate sense of pain that accompanies separation. But the meaningful exercise of discipline must include the possibility of separation.

Divisions that emerge out of conflicting understandings of the gospel are not inherently evil. They may serve to remind us of the richness of God's work in the world. The multiplicity of denominations and subgroups within the Anabaptist-Mennonite tradition, for example, challenge the claims of any single group to have a monopoly on God's truth. I, for one, deeply appreciate the witness that the Amish represent amidst the fragmenting juggernaut of modernity. The three million people who travel annually to northern Indiana don't come because of the Mennonites—General Conference, "Old" Mennonite, or otherwise. They come because they recognize in the Amish a way of life that stands in sharp contrast to their own and that prompts them to view in a new light the apparent inevitabilities of modern individualism and consumerism. We are all richer for them, and for the particularity offered by other groups in the Anabaptist-Mennonite tradition.

The boundaries of the gathered church—forged by our commitments of mutual love and vulnerability—offer a genuine alternative to a world defined by alienation, isolation, and loneliness. Let us be good stewards of this treasure that has been handed down to us.

2

Historical Contexts for MC–GC Integration: Franconia Conference Split (1847) and Russian Migration (1874)

James Juhnke

At least two polarities are foundational for understanding the historical context of Mennonite Church–General Conference Mennonite Church integration. One is the difference between "new" Mennonites and "old" Mennonites, a distinction that resulted from a schism in the Franconia Conference in 1847. Another is the difference between Mennonites who trace their ancestry to the Swiss and South German region of the Anabaptist movement, and those who trace their ancestry to the Dutch and North German region of the movement.[1]

We all see the past in terms of who and where we are in the present. The 1847 Oberholzer schism in the Franconia Conference in Pennsylvania, and the 1860 founding of the General Conference Mennonite Church in West Point, Iowa, were events in the Swiss–South German stream of Anabaptist-Mennonitism. Those of us who come out of this Pennsylvania-German heritage are more or less comfortable with this historical context for MC–GC unity discussions. What seems to be happening is the attempted healing of a split that goes back to 1847.

Those of us from west of the Mississippi River and from Ontario westward in Canada, who are descendants of the 1870s, 1920s, and 1940s migrants from Russia and eastern Europe, have a different perspective. The Dutch-Russian tradition goes back in a direct line to the

---

[1] I attempted to summarize the differences between these two streams in "Mennonite History and Self-Understanding: North American Mennonitism as a Bipolar Mosaic," in *Mennonite Identity: Historical and Contemporary Perspectives,* ed. Calvin Wall Redekop and Samuel J. Steiner (Lanham, Md.: University Press of America, 1988), 83–99. This bipolar model was foundational for my volume in the Mennonite Experience in America (MEA) project (vol. 3), *Vision, Doctrine, War: Mennonite Identity and Organization in America 1890–1930* (Scottdale, Pa., and Waterloo, Ont.: Herald Press, 1989).

sixteenth-century Reformation by way of immigrant ancestors from eastern Europe. Folk from this tradition feel strange when they are defined in terms of John Oberholzer and the Franconia schism of 1847. From the Dutch-Russian perspective, the prospect of MC–GC unity means the partial merging of streams that began separately in different parts of Europe more than four and a half centuries ago.

The development of ecclesiastical forms has been complex for all sides of these two polarities, and Mennonite denominational historians have not done a notably thorough or rigorous job of explaining the developments. In the latter decades of the twentieth century, the two major historical projects have been the four-volume series on The Mennonite Experience in America,[2] and the three-volume history of Mennonites in Canada.[3] If you look for the word "polity" in the indexes of these seven volumes, you will find it only in volume 2 of the MEA series, by Theron Schlabach. The historians' relative inattention to issues of church polity is most remarkable given the growing popular use of that concept in recent years among our people. Our deficit of historical information and understanding is partly due to the complexities and inconsistencies in historical Mennonite and Amish church developments. Much church discipline is informal, the result of collectively raised eyebrows more than of actions written down for historians to discover. We do not have enough local studies to help us sort out the difference between official polity statements and what happened in practice.[4]

---

[2] Richard MacMaster, *Land, Piety, Peoplehood: The Establishment of Mennonite Communities in America 1683–1790*, MEA, vol. 1 (Scottdale, Pa., and Kitchener, Ont.: Herald Press, 1985); Theron F. Schlabach, *Peace, Faith, Nation: Mennonites and Amish in Nineteenth-Century America*, MEA, vol. 2 (Scottdale, Pa., and Kitchener, Ont.: Herald Press, 1988); Juhnke, *Vision, Doctrine, War*; Paul Toews, *Mennonites in American Society 1930–1970: Modernity and the Persistence of Religious Community*, MEA, vol. 4 (Scottdale, Pa., and Waterloo, Ont.: Herald Press, 1996).

[3] Frank H. Epp, *Mennonites in Canada, 1786–1920: The History of a Separate People* ([Altona, Man.]: Mennonite Historical Society of Canada, 1990); Frank H. Epp, *Mennonites in Canada, 1920–1940: A People's Struggle for Survival* (Toronto: Macmillan of Canada; and Scottdale, Pa.: Herald Press, 1982); T. D. Regehr, *Mennonites in Canada, 1939–1970: A People Transformed* (Toronto: University of Toronto Press, 1996).

[4] There is a helpful summary, based mostly on official statements, in section two of *A Mennonite Polity for Ministerial Leadership*, ed. Everett J. Thomas (Newton, Kans.: Faith and Life Press, 1996), 32–72.

In this paper I will not attempt to do what Mennonite historians have neglected to do in the last three decades. I have done no fresh research. I can only attempt to offer historical context by way of some information about the Franconia schism of 1847 and the Dutch-Russian migration of the 1870s.

FRANCONIA, OBERHOLZER, AND THE GENERAL CONFERENCE

The Franconia schism of 1847 cast a long and pervasive shadow. Few events in North American Mennonite history have been subjected to such thorough and insightful scholarly investigation. The most impressive treatments are by J. C. Wenger,[5] Leland Harder,[6] S. F. Pannabecker,[7] John L. Ruth,[8] Beulah Hostetler,[9] and Theron Schlabach.[10] In 1847, John H. Oberholzer was a thirty-nine-year-old schoolteacher and pastor of the Swamp Mennonite Congregation in Bucks County, Pennsylvania. He led a movement in which all or parts of fourteen congregations, a total of about five hundred persons, left the Franconia Conference to form the East Pennsylvania Mennonite Conference. As John Ruth has written, for a decade pressure had been building in Franconia churches for "more congregationalism, less emphasis on 'externals,' more openness to the surrounding culture, and a new independent body."[11] When the break came, the main public issues seemed to be the prescribed plain coat for ministers, a constitution, and the recording of official minutes. But the underlying issues were more profound. As Theron Schlabach tells the

---

[5] John C. Wenger, *History of the Mennonites of the Franconia Conference* (Telford, Pa.: Franconia Mennonite Historical Society, 1937).

[6] Leland Harder, "The Quest for Equilibrium in an Established Sect: A Study of Social Change in the General Conference Mennonite Church" (Ann Arbor, Mich.: University Microfilms, 1976).

[7] Samuel Floyd Pannabecker, *Open Doors: The History of the General Conference Mennonite Church* (Newton, Kans.: Faith and Life Press, 1975), 10–38.

[8] John L. Ruth, *Maintaining the Right Fellowship: A Narrative Account of Life in the Oldest Mennonite Community in North America* (Scottdale, Pa.: Herald Press, 1984), 232–77.

[9] Beulah Stauffer Hostetler, *American Mennonites and Protestant Movements: A Community Paradigm* (Scottdale, Pa.: Herald Press, 1987), 125–49.

[10] Schlabach, *Peace, Faith, Nation*, 117–40.

[11] Ruth, *Maintaining the Right Fellowship*, 231.

story, at stake were the core values of humility and submission as well as traditional notions of authority in the church.[12]

In recent years, the Mennonite scholars' interpretation of the Franconia division has undergone a substantial shift. An earlier generation, the mid-twentieth-century builders of Mennonite denominational institutions, such as E. G. Kaufman and H. S. Bender, believed that nineteenth-century Mennonitism went through a "dark age" followed by a "great awakening." As the twentieth-century institution builders saw it, early-nineteenth-century Mennonite leaders were uneducated and unenlightened traditionalists who knew of little beyond the cultural boundaries they rigorously defended. But then came a generation of enlightened progressives, men such as John Oberholzer and John F. Funk, who led the way toward a more progressive piety and toward aggressive outward ministries of education, publication, missionary endeavor, and conference organization.

More recently a cohort of neo-conservative Mennonite scholars have revised the "dark ages to great awakening" thesis. These scholars have taken a freshly appreciative look at what Beulah Hostetler has called the traditional Mennonite "charter."[13] The charter was partly written and partly unwritten, a core of foundational values, practices, and traditions that survived to sustain community identity and morale in the face of swirling challenges from the outside. In American democratic society the challenges to Mennonite ways were relentless. Among them were revivalism, individualism, militarism, reformist optimism, and the lure of denominational institutional development. In the neo-conservative revision, nineteenth-century Mennonite progressives were not portrayed as far-seeing apostles of enlightenment. They rather were unwitting victims of outside forces they did not understand and could not control. Theron Schlabach, for example, used language of pathology to describe the founders of Wadsworth Institute in 1868 as carriers of "a college-building fever that had many denominations in its grip."[14] Schlabach's rhetoric almost seems to imply that this fever was a social equivalent of epidemic smallpox, with entire tribes falling victim.

The Franconia division was in 1847. The founding of the General Conference Mennonite Church came thirteen years later, in 1860.

---

[12] Schlabach, *Peace, Faith, Nation*, 119–21.

[13] Hostetler, *American Mennonites*, 75–77.

[14] Schlabach, *Peace, Faith, Nation*, 132.

Contrary to what we might expect, these events were not closely connected. Recently-arrived South German immigrants on the frontier in Lee County, Iowa (not Oberholzer and his circle from Franconia), called the first meeting of the General Conference. Only two delegates from outside Iowa were present. Oberholzer himself would not have attended except that someone paid his way at the last minute. Yet this handful of immigrants audaciously created a union intended to embrace all Mennonites of North America. They planned to engage in common work of education, publication, and missions, but not to require uniformity in what they considered "nonessentials."

The new General Conference unity movement had limited success in attracting members from among Mennonites who had been in North America longer and were organized into the regional conferences of Franconia, Lancaster, Ontario, Virginia, Washington-Franklin, Ohio, and Indiana. By 1875, fifteen years after its beginning, the ambitious new GC body had only twenty-three congregations. Total membership was just 1,440 persons. Why did American "old" Mennonites resist the GC progressive plan for union? Theron Schlabach's explanation is persuasive: "Old" Mennonites would hardly rush to accept the leadership of recent German immigrants in the West, especially if the controversial Oberholzer was connected to the movement and if the immigrant founders' commitment to charter values was suspect. "Old" Mennonites who were interested in progressive change (a minority in the mid-to-late nineteenth century) were more inclined to follow a leader such as John F. Funk. Funk was a child of Franconia who had gone west but had not forgotten his roots. He knew better than the recent immigrants in Iowa how to combine the new reforms with "the old humility- and nonresistant-gospel symbols, idiom and theology."[15] In 1864, in Elkhart, Funk began publishing the *Herald of Truth* and *Der Herold der Wahrheit*, with much the same denominational activist agenda that the immigrant GC founders had claimed in Iowa. But it required great patience. Not until 1898 did the "old" Mennonites organize their own general conference. Even then the conservative district conferences of Franconia and Lancaster withheld formal membership from the wider body.

---

[15] Schlabach, *Peace, Faith, Nation*, 139.

THE COMING OF THE RUSSIAN MENNONITES

Until the 1870s, nearly all European Mennonite immigrants to North America came from the Swiss and South German stream of Anabaptist-Mennonitism. There had been a few Dutch or North German immigrants, but they had been culturally co-opted into the Pennsylvania German mainstream or into other American traditions. In the 1870s and 1880s, some 18,000 Mennonites of Dutch and North German background, including about a third of the Mennonites in Russia, migrated to North America. Although these migrants came from geographically-separated communities in eastern Europe, they all had a strong sense of Mennonite cultural identity. They all knew how to maintain their group boundaries over against non-Mennonites. One boundary marker was their Low German dialect, which precisely marked the border of Mennonite community. American Mennonites, in contrast, shared the Pennsylvania German dialect with their non-Mennonite neighbors.

The ruling autocrats of the Russian Empire had granted Mennonite communities substantial political and cultural autonomy. Mennonite villagers in Russia remembered a past of persecution and had internalized a mentality of humble submission typical of a tenuously tolerated sect. But in Russia they had opportunity to learn the arts and practices of self-government at the local level. After their migration to the North American frontier, these Mennonites were more inclined to accept responsibility for religious-secular institutions of community development. In Kansas, for example, they soon established three institutions that had no clear counterpart among American Mennonites of Swiss and South German background: (1) Mennonite-edited German-language newspapers, quasi-denominational, with both secular and religious content; (2) a German Teacher's Association for the teachers in Mennonite parochial schools; and (3) the deaconess hospital, which combined male entrepreneurial energies with female idealistic voluntarism, in health care institutional development.

In our current MC–GC unity discussions, we should note that the immigrants of the 1870s and 1880s had three options for denominational organization in North America. (1) They could have formed regional district conferences in the West as they settled, developed informal associational ties with John F. Funk's American "old" Mennonites, and then in 1898 joined the MC conference. (2) They could have joined the General Conference Mennonite Church as individual congregations, associating with the GC Western District, which included congregations from New York to Kansas. (3) They could have organized their separate bodies and kept themselves institutionally apart from Mennonites of other ethnic backgrounds.

Some of the immigrants, most notably the Mennonite Brethren, the Krimmer Mennonite Brethren, and the Evangelical Mennonite Brethren, chose option 3 and organized their own separate, ethnically homogeneous bodies. In Kansas, many immigrant congregations organized a separate Kansas Conference of Mennonites in 1877. Some of those congregations also joined the General Conference Mennonite Church as individual congregations. In 1892, the entire regional Kansas Conference of Mennonites joined the GCs, choosing option 2. Almost none of the immigrants chose option 1, that is, to join the "old" Mennonites. The Evangelical Mennonite Brethren did carry on an extended flirtation with the "old" Mennonites, which resulted in the anomaly of missionaries named Friesen serving with the MC mission in India. But the EMB–MC unity effort ultimately failed.[16]

Why did most of the Dutch-Russian immigrants join the General Conference rather than the "old" Mennonites? Most important, I believe, was the GC missionary work. The example of the Alexanderwohl congregation, largest and most influential of the immigrant groups, set a pattern for others. Heinrich H. Richert, Alexanderwohl elder, was a strong supporter of overseas missions. He was a friend and correspondent of Heinrich Dirks, Russian Mennonite missionary in Sumatra under the Dutch mission board. In 1876, barely two years after settling in Kansas, Richert attended a meeting of the Western District of the General Conference in Halstead, Kansas. That meeting led to Richert's election to the General Conference mission board. One youthful Alexanderwohl member, Heinrich R. Voth (Richert's nephew), had felt a calling to missionary service already before the 1874 migration. After arriving in Kansas, Voth wrote to John F. Funk in Elkhart about his missions interest. Funk replied that the American Mennonites did not have overseas missions program; he should inquire with the Dutch Mennonite board in Amsterdam. Voth then turned to the General Conference, studied at the school in Wadsworth, and became a GCMC missionary to the American Indians.[17] In 1878, when the large Alexanderwohl congregation joined the struggling General Conference Mennonite Church, their addition increased the conference membership

---

[16] Juhnke, *Vision, Doctrine, War*, 47–49, 100.

[17] James C. Juhnke, *A People of Mission: A History of General Conference Mennonite Overseas Missions* (Newton, Kans.: Faith and Life Press, 1979), 7–8.

by twenty-four percent.[18] Other immigrant congregations followed on the strength of their interest in denominational missions and education.

Theron Schlabach listed "congregationalism" as his first reason why the GCMC won so many of the Russian immigrants. The GCMC was congregationalist while the "old" Mennonites were "quite synodical." Schlabach's point is insightful and, I think, also potentially misleading. He wrote:

> The GCs succeeded by using their central structures mainly for program while leaving discipline and intensity of fellowship to congregations. So their structures allowed flexibility and variety. "Old" and Amish Mennonites had grasped one horn of a persistent Christian dilemma: the principle that God's people really should present the world with a clear, common, corporate voice and example. The GC Mennonites chose the other horn (the horn on which American denominationalism also hung): the principle of mutual acceptance, tolerance, cooperation, and more Christian freedom.... That strategy allowed immigrant and American Mennonites to come together with considerable freedom for different traditions.[19]

Yes, the GCMC, formed in 1860, had a congregationalist polity. But it is less clear that the Dutch-Russian immigrants in the late nineteenth century were committed congregationalists. More research needs to be done on this topic.[20] James Urry has argued that the local areas became like parishes. "In the start they were Flemish or Frisian but scattered through villages. Then Frisians and Flemish faded and they became Kirchliche.... The relation of Elder to ministers is crucial here and the task was incomplete."[21] Apparently some elders oversaw a number of satellite worship groups or congregations, although an elder could also be in charge of a single congregation. In the United States, the

---

[18] Leland Harder, *General Conference Mennonite Church Fact Book of Congregational Membership* (Leland Harder, 1971), 3.

[19] Schlabach, *Peace, Faith, Nation,* 284.

[20] Steven Nolt has written, "They championed congregationalism...." (in "Ethnicity and North American Mennonites," *The Mennonite* [June 22, 1999], 4–5), and Robert Kreider has spoken of the Dutch-Russian immigrant "commitment to congregational polity" ("Did Not Our Hearts Burn within Us? Reflections at the End of a Journey," unpublished text of speech given at joint MC–GC conference in St. Louis, July 1999).

[21] James Urry, email message to the author, August 2, 1999. James.Urry@vuw.ac.nz.

institution of the "bishop district" emerged as one leader exercised authority over offshoot congregations. How did these patterns of authority change over time? I don't know. In Canada, the Bergthal Mennonites and the Rudnerweide Mennonites of the 1870s migration developed or extended a system in which one elder had authority over multiple congregations and ministers.[22] In Kansas, the elder of the Hoffnungsau Mennonite congregation had authority over offshoot or satellite congregations in Inman (1909) and Buhler (1920). Ten years later, in 1920 and 1921, when the Buhler and Inman groups formed separate congregations, they did not ordain separate elders.

The resolutions of the Kansas Conference of Mennonites, a separate and unaffiliated conference formed by immigrants of 1877, suggest that these people were not unqualified champions of a congregational polity. In 1886 a new congregation, which had split from the original Mennonite church in Newton, applied for conference membership. The Kansas Conference rejected their application and identified four problem areas. The new congregation (1) did not prohibit members from belonging to secret societies, (2) was willing to accept members who had been baptized as infants, (3) needed to move to ensure that its minister/elder was ordained by an "established and recognized" elder, and (4) needed to repair its conflict with the first Mennonite Church of Newton. At the same time, the conference record insisted that "the tendency of our Conference endeavors is a uniting one and not a separating one...."[23] This may have been congregationalism of a type, but the Kansas Conference decision of 1886 (reaffirmed the following year) set a standard on the stated issues for all member congregations.

Our currently popular notion that the 1870s immigrants from Russia were congregationalist may have arisen in part from a misinterpretation of the ideas of Cornelius H. Wedel, the most articulate spokesman of this group until his death in 1910. My own writing may have contributed to

---

[22] *The Mennonite Encyclopedia* (Hillsboro, Kans.: Mennonite Brethren Publishing House; Newton, Kans.: Mennonite Publication Office; Scottdale, Pa.: Mennonite Publishing House, 1955), 1:280-81.

[23] Kansas Conference Minutes, translation, 1886. John D. Thiesen, *Prussian Roots, Kansas Branches: A History of First Mennonite Church of Newton* (Newton, Kans.: Historical Committee of First Mennonite Church, 1986), 38-39. David A. Haury, *Prairie People: A History of the Western District Conference* (Newton, Kans.: Faith and Life Press, 1981), 177.

this misunderstanding.[24] Wedel made the *Gemeinde* (congregation) the central concept for his interpretation of Anabaptist and Mennonite history. He spoke of Mennonites as a *Gemeindekirche,* and Mennonitism as *Gemeindechristentum.* These are not easy concepts to translate into English. Translators have often imputed more individualism and autonomy to the concept than Wedel intended. For example, in 1903, Wedel described Anabaptist communities as follows: "Da haben wir eine Gemeindekirche vor uns, wo alle kirchlichen Entscheidungen von dem Amt am Wort und der Gemeinde getroffen wurden." In 1926, Wedel's son Theodore translated that sentence: "We find instead a local congregational government in which the ministers and the congregation itself made decisions."[25]

The result of this translation is a more specific implication of local congregationalist polity than Wedel intended. The context of Wedel's characterization here of *Gemeindekirche* is broad, a general contrast with the Old Testament *Priesterkirche* and with the Roman Empire's *Staatskirche.* In fact, Wedel never advocated the autonomy of local congregations. In the 1903 book quoted above, Wedel also wrote, in a passage identifying some historical weaknesses of the Mennonite tradition: "Das demokratische Prinzip unserer Gemeinschaft ließ es oft zu den allernötigsten Vereinigungen nicht kommen. Der Independentismus lähmte das Streben nach einheitlicher Gesinnung und einheitlichem Wirken."[26] Such a statement, of course, is a critique of unqualified congregationalism. Wedel's concept of *Gemeinde* deserves further study.

Wedel's Kansas community, the regional expression of what he called *Gemeindechristentum,* was organized into ethnically homogeneous congregations. Nearly all were run by close networks of

---

[24] James C. Juhnke, *Vision Doctrine, War,* 101–5.

[25] C. H. Wedel, *Geleitworte an junge Christen. Zunächst in unsern mennonitischen Kreisen* (Newton, Kans.: Schulverlag von Bethel College, 1903), 27; *Words to Young Christians: Particularly to Those of the Mennonite Church,* trans. Theodore O. Wedel (Berne, Ind.: The Mennonite Book Concern, 1926), 32.

[26] Wedel, *Geleitworte,* 36. Theodore Wedel translated this passage as follows: "The principle of church democracy has been overemphasized, thus preventing often the most necessary unity of effort. Attempts at spiritual approach or joint activity were crippled by stressing congregational independence" (*Words to Young Christians,* 42).

related families. Yet many of these congregations had come from different parts of eastern Europe and south Russia, and they had different customs and church practices. I would propose, subject to further research and correction, that these Kansas Conference congregations in their new environment opted for a more congregational polity because they had to accommodate cultural differences, rather than because they were accustomed to a congregational polity before they left eastern Europe. Moreover, as a group of congregations, none of which used the Pennsylvania-German dialect typical of "old" Mennonites, they were different from Mennonites who had been in America for some generations. It was probably their ethnic cultural differences from the American "old" Mennonites (and, to some extent, their differences from each other), rather than their congregationalism, that pushed them away from quasi-synodical Swiss–South German "old" Mennonites and toward the congregationalist Swiss–South German GCMC.

What happens to separate-from-the-world groups that invest major energies, in Schlabach's words, to "present the world with a clear, common, corporate voice and example"? They present that example not only to the world but also to their brothers and sisters in the faith who have different cultural means of group identification. The "old" Mennonite quasi-synodical, bishop-led polity, in its drive for consensus and consistency, resulted in rules and practices that seemed strange to the immigrant Dutch-Russians. The immigrants had their own means of group boundary maintenance and gospel faithfulness. It is not clear that in their European communities of immigrant origin they had failed to "present the world with a clear, common, corporate voice and example."

Nevertheless, in America these immigrants found themselves not in conformity with the cultural standards, rooted in the gospel, of American Mennonites of Swiss and South German background. "Old" Mennonites quite understandably saw an absence of "humility" and an evidence of worldly pride in such things as the immigrants' non-regulation preacher's coats, the type of head coverings worn by the women, or placement of the pulpit in worship spaces. The immigrants were understandably drawn to affiliate with other Mennonites who did not challenge their own time-honored folkways. The congregationalism of the original GCMC was a mechanism for accommodating cultural differences. But their winning of the immigrants was not necessarily a marriage of two different streams of congregationalist polity. This question deserves further research and analysis.

Merging Streams

What can the study of history contribute to MC–GC unity discussions? At the least, we need to learn to listen to each other's stories. Good storytelling and story-listening depends on imaginative comprehension of the ethnic and cultural background of the actors and tellers of the stories. Inheritors of the Dutch-Russian stream need to go to Pennsylvania and learn about Oberholzer and the Franconia schism of 1847. They should read the historical accounts by John Ruth; the novel by Sara Stambaugh, *I Hear the Reaper's Song*;[27] and the many resources that help explain how the Amish have had strong impact on MC Mennonite consciousness. They should not see the MC or "old" Mennonites as people somehow lacking the cultural substance and pathos of true Dutch-Russian Mennonitism.

By the same token, inheritors of the Swiss–South German stream need to go beyond the Mississippi River, or perhaps to Winnipeg, and learn to know the Mennonites there. They should read the novels of Rudy Wiebe, Al Reimer, and Dallas Wiebe. They should understand that these Dutch-Russians are not first and foremost descendants of John Oberholzer, not somehow breakaways from an Anabaptism that began with Conrad Grebel in Zurich. The Dutch-Russians are inheritors and representatives of an Anabaptist-Mennonite tradition that has its own story.

As far as ecclesiology is concerned, in my view, it is helpful to recognize that both of these traditions in the North American twentieth-century context have generally moved in the direction of a congregational polity, at different times and for different reasons. We still do not understand fully how this happened, but better knowledge of these matters will contribute to mutual cooperation and union.

---

[27] Sara Stambaugh, *I Hear the Reaper's Song* (Intercourse, Pa.: Good Books, 1984).

3

Marks of the Church in Galatians: Inheriting a Map without Territory

Jo-Ann Brant

In his 1974 essay, "Map Is Not Territory," Jonathan Z. Smith issued a now normative warning that religious scholars and scholars of religion tend to map religious space based on a propensity to dichotomize the world "into the 'we' and the 'them,'" a propensity that "has resulted in much mischief."[1] Current discourse frequently accuses us of doing much worse.

Smith's warning is to be heeded at several levels. The writers of the New Testament were cartographers working from a map that once described a physical territory. They used this map to demarcate the sacred geography of Christianity that exists only as social space. The boundaries they drew between pure and impure or Jew and Gentile appeared to the authors to be identifiable lines, but we go astray if we use them to orient ourselves to Mediterranean territory in the Greco-Roman era. Our sense of direction becomes even more confused when we use their map to take our bearings in our own society. They used the criterion of true worship versus idolatry to draw the map of antiquity, and applied the word "idolatry" to pagan social space. We frequently apply the category of idolatry metaphorically to secular social space.

Rather than rejecting maps, Smith challenges us to "undergo the ordeal of incongruity."[2] The following discussion of Paul's letter to the Galatians and, secondarily, of his first letter to the Corinthians, takes up that challenge. In Galatians Paul appropriates the map of Judaism, and in 1 Corinthians he places that map on Gentile territory. By attending closely to how Paul interprets and orients his scriptural map, we may find it possible to avoid the mischief or violence of the past while

---

[1] Jonathan Z. Smith, "Map Is Not Territory," in *Map Is Not Territory: Studies in the History of Religions* (Leiden: E. J. Brill, 1978), 294. Smith borrows his title from the dictum of philosopher of semantics Alfred Korzybski.

[2] Ibid., 309.

negotiating our situation and thereby defining the space in which we dwell.

The New Testament does not reject the map the Old Testament provides; it uses that map to renegotiate who is included in God's realm by superimposing the map on what Paul identifies as a new creation.[3] The salvation of the Exodus—the deliverance from bondage in Israel to the inheritance of the land promised in Genesis—becomes the movement from life in the old creation to life in the new creation. The boundary between the sacred and the profane, between true worship and idolatry, drawn on the Old Testament landscape, with the temple in Jerusalem as God's dwelling place, ceases to be physical space and becomes social space. God dwells within the *ecclesia* of Christ (1 Cor. 3:16). In the Old Testament, the deuteronomic curse unleashed by disobedience (Deut. 27:15–26), to which Paul refers in Gal. 3:10, entails the loss of the land and a return to Egypt (Deut. 28:64–68). Membership in the people of God is made visible by the mark of circumcision upon the male body. For Paul, the terrain of freedom becomes life in Christ, a social space produced by the indwelling of Christ within the one who lives by faith (Gal. 2:19–20).[4] The zones of purity surround the human body, now described as the temple (1 Cor. 6:19), a description that perhaps gives greater gravity to the defilement of sexual violations (cf. 1 Cor. 6:16–18; Gal. 5:19). Circumcision becomes the invisible mark inscribed on one's heart, a matter of spirit, not flesh (Rom. 2:28).

While Paul asserts that "neither circumcision nor uncircumcision is anything; but a new creation is everything!" (Gal. 6:15), he persists in conceiving of a world that is distinguished by Jew and Gentile, true worshiper and idolater. He imposes a unified social identity, sometimes that of Gentile, sometimes that of Greek, on a world that would find such

---

[3] As Henri Lefebvre points out with reference to the Roman appropriation of Greek theology, "adoption of another's gods always entails the adoption of their space and system of measurement" (Henri Lefebvre, *The Production of Space*, trans. Donald Nicholson-Smith [Oxford: Basil Blackwell, 1991], 111).

[4] According to Don Garlington, "Role Reversal and Paul's Use of Scripture in Galatians 3.10–13" *Journal for the Study of the New Testament* 65 (March 1997): 98–99, the language of the LXX which Paul adopts signifies "remaining within a specified territory." J. Christiaan Beker confirms that "in Christ" has a "local and an instrumental meaning." "In Christ" signifies the language of incorporation (Johan Christiaan Beker, *Paul the Apostle: The Triumph of God in Life and Thought* [Philadelphia: Fortress Press, 1980], 272).

a designation meaningless.⁵ Ironically, before one could assent to the truth of Paul's conviction that there is neither Jew nor Greek, one had to begin to see oneself as a part of the dichotomy that Paul rejects.

In the new creation, the realm of idolatry is obliterated; consequently, there is neither Jew nor Gentile. The problem with which Paul must contend, or, in more positive terms, the opportunity for a mission to the Gentiles that the delay of the *parousia* affords, is the persistence of the physical reality. As a result, boundaries must be drawn to differentiate the realm of true worship from the realm of idolatry. Normative rules of morality must be established. Paul removes ritual barriers to worship—circumcision, in particular—but Torah continues to play a role in defining the circumference of territory.⁶ The heat of the Torah/*Nomos* debate waged by Pauline scholars during the last century is sufficient evidence that Paul's treatment of the law admits incongruity. While scholars struggle to understand the criteria for Paul's positive and negative statements about the law, Christians have considered various laws binding, whatever Paul's intent. Christians reading the map discern that Paul draws a fuzzy line between the moral purity and the ritual purity demanded by the law.⁷ Paul's ambiguous treatment of the law allows Christianity to define normative behavior within the church but permits mischief when Christians appropriate moral purity as an identity marker.

While the sacred geography of the Mosaic covenant draws clear lines between purity and impurity, it does not necessarily define the realm of those things we tend to identify with moral purity as coterminous with the realm of purity. Second Temple Judaism was capable of recognizing the righteous Gentile, someone who lives in impurity but is righteous. While Paul seems to draw from this tradition in

---

⁵ Terence L. Donaldson, *Paul and the Gentiles: Remapping the Apostle's Convictional World* (Minneapolis: Fortress Press, 1997), 159.

⁶ See Troy Martin, "Pagan and Judeo-Christian Time-Keeping Schemes in Gal 4.10 and Col 2.16," *New Testament Studies* 42 (January 1996): 105–119, for a discussion of Paul's retention of the Hebraic calendar.

⁷ Any use of this distinction must be qualified with the understanding that it is imposed upon the tradition. We definitely err if we draw a distinction between natural law and positive law or seek some sort of Kantian universal ethic. The ethic of the Hebrew Scriptures is God's revealed will. See Ephraim E. Urbach,, *The Sages, Their Concepts and Beliefs* (Cambridge: Harvard University Press, 1987), 313–23, for an extension of the argument to the Tannaim and Amoraim.

his argument in Rom. 2:14–15, he alters the landscape. Whereas in the Old Testament and Judaism, idolatry by those within the covenant is treated metaphorically as adultery, and hence as an immoral act, foreign worship by those outside the covenant can be seen as error.[8] The talmudic rabbis were free to draw distinctions such as the following: "Gentiles outside the Land of Israel are not idolaters, but they are merely following the custom of ancestors" (*b. Hul* 13b). Paul retains the association of idolatry with sexual licentiousness but wrenches it loose from its context within the covenant. In Galatians, he underscores the fact that idolatry is not simply the worship of gods that are no gods, by stating that it is partnership or bondage with "weak beggarly elemental spirits" (Gal. 4:9). In 1 Corinthians, he calls pagan worship partnership with demons (1 Cor. 10:20–22), and links sexual immorality and idolatry (1 Cor. 10:6–8; cf. also 1 Cor. 5:1).[9] Consequently, Christianity has had difficulty finding room in its cosmology for an individual analogous to the righteous Gentile.

Whereas Paul is dealing with a highly abstract cosmology, Christians have done mischief by using the map to read the landscape of the historical world of antiquity and describing those who are not Christian as the immoral. Post-holocaust studies have drawn our attention to a long and ignoble tradition, beginning with the church fathers and extending to the present, in which Jews have been accused of all that is wicked.[10] Perhaps, because paganism was officially abolished in 391 C.E., we are less sensitive to the perpetuation of the tendency to

---

[8] Moshe Halbertal and Avishai Margalit, *Idolatry*, trans. Naomi Goldblum (Cambridge: Harvard University Press, 1992), 116.

[9] Ibid., 185.

[10] See, for example, St. John Chrysostom *Homilies against the Jews* 1:4: "Of their rapine, their cupidity, their deception of the pen, of thievery, and huckstering? Indeed a whole day would not suffice to tell all." "Lustful rapacious, greedy perfidious bandits, ...inveterate murderers," guilty of "debauchery and drunkenness," they "have surpassed the ferocity of the wild beasts for they murder their offspring and immolate them to the devil.... They are impure and impious." D. B. Garlington, "Hierosylein and the Idolatry of Israel (Romans 2:22)," *New Testament Studies* 36 (January 1990): 148, uses milder terms but betrays the same tendency when he argues that Jews become idolaters by making the law an idol. In my Sunday school class, on Sunday, January 9, 2000, I heard the statement, "There is no forgiveness or grace in Judaism."

characterize the Gentile as morally impure. For example, Paul's map is frequently read as though it described the actual territory of Corinth. In *The New Testament in its Social Environment,* John E. Stambaugh and David L. Balch write, "Most Greeks did not perceive any immorality in prostitution...and Paul's polemic against sexual excess (1 Corinthians 5–7) is addressed to Corinthian Christians who had in the local spirit coined the slogan 'All things are lawful for me' (1 Cor. 6:12)."[11]

Would a Corinthian recognize himself or herself in this portrait? Negative treatments of Corinthian piety tend to focus on the worship of Aphrodite. The phrase "the rites of Aphrodite" is a euphemism for lovemaking (Achilles Tatius *Leucippe and Clitophon* 4.1), and Athenaeus's satire, *The Deipnosophistai,* makes Aphrodite the patroness of a guild of prostitutes. But more serious ancient sources reveal that Aphrodite was worshiped as the patroness of marriage and family life.[12] Even the ancient Greek novels—the racy parts of which are translated into Latin in the first Loeb editions to encourage young boys to extend

---

[11] John E. Stambaugh and David L. Balch, *The New Testament in Its Social Environment* (Philadelphia: Westminster Press, 1986), 158. Jerome Murphy-O'Connor, *Saint Paul's Corinth: Texts and Archaeology* (Wilmington: Michael Glazier, 1983), provides an extensive treatment of the primary sources with which scholarship can reconstruct a picture of Corinthian society. He warns that "sacred prostitution was never a Greek custom and, were Corinth an exception, the silence of all other ancient [sources] becomes impossible to explain" (56). He also cites Hans Conzelmann's conclusion that the treatment of Corinth as a place of sexual promiscuity is "Athenian propaganda" (57). Many New Testament scholars who use Murphy-O'Connor's book fail to heed his warning about the nature of these sources. See Kevin Quast, *Reading the Corinthian Correspondence: An Introduction* (New York: Paulist Press, 1994), 20, for a characterization of first-century Corinth based on Plato's *Republic.* See Charles H. Talbert, *Reading Corinthians* (New York: Crossroad, 1987), 31, for a characterization of Gentile use of prostitution based on Philo of Alexandria and Josephus. See Graydon F. Snyder, *First Corinthians: A Faith Community Commentary* (Macon: Mercer University Press, 1992), 2, for a characterization based on Aristophanes.

[12] Strabo *Geography* 8.6.20, describes Corinth's past, not what he himself observes, when he describes temple prostitutes. In Pausanias's description of Corinth, 11.26–11.33 (ca. 155 C.E.), we find the description of temples and orderly worship. Cf. Lynn R. LiDonnici, "Women's Religions and Religious Lives in the Greco-Roman City," in *Women and Christian Origins,* ed. Ross Shepard Kraemer and Mary Rose D'Angelo (New York: Oxford University Press, 1999), 82–83.

their study of the classical languages—reveal a world that values chastity and sanctifies marriage.[13] Leucippe, heroine of Achilles Tatius's novel, obeying the goddess Artemis who guards her virginity, meets her seducer with the following words: "Bring on the instruments of torture: the wheel—here, take my arms and stretch them; the whips—here is my back, lash away; the hot irons—here is my body for burning; bring the axe as well—here is my neck, slice through. Watch a new contest: a single woman competes with all the engines of torture and wins every round" (6.21).[14] Compare this to Susanna's response to seduction: "I am completely trapped. For if I do this, it will mean death for me; if I do not, I cannot escape your hands. I choose not to do it; I will fall into your hands, rather than sin in the sight of the Lord" (Sus. 1:22-23). Susanna fears the consequences of infidelity; Leucippe honors virtue.

Paul may not have intended that such mischief be done, but his quick rhetorical skips—from circumcision, to flesh, to fleshly sins, to the realm of sin, to worship of other gods—indicate that Paul differentiates the realm of true worship from false worship on moral grounds. The mistake that we make is to lay Paul's map on the ancient world and thereby generate a false "we" and "them" dichotomy. If we muster the imagination to lay it on the new creation, the map may become less problematic and even compelling.

Paul argues that he has died to the law and therefore is no longer under the law. It is possible that he bases this argument on a prior understanding of the jurisdiction of the law. Later rabbinic traditions state that one is exempt from observance of precepts when one enters the realm of death (*b. Sabbat* 151b). The tradition of the *Bat Qol*, which does not allow a voice from heaven to influence a ruling, affirms an understanding running through the rabbinic material that the Torah is given to the Israelites and it is theirs to interpret and apply in life.[15] Like Jesus, who is condemned by the law (Gal. 3:13), the verdict of which has no jurisdiction in the resurrection, Paul, who is crucified in Christ, no longer comes under the jurisdiction of the law. Given that the categories of abstract social space in Christianity are contingent on the world that Torah defines—its purity, its holiness, its genealogy—Paul does not

---

[13] See Kate Cooper, *The Virgin and the Bride: Idealized Womanhood in Late Antiquity* (Cambridge: Harvard University Press, 1996), 19.

[14] Achilles Tatius *Leucippe and Clitophon* 6.21, in *Collected Ancient Greek Novels*, ed. B. P. Reardon (Berkeley: University of California Press, 1989), 259.

[15] For example, see *Sipra Be-huqqotay* 8.

intend that Christians may be ignorant of the law just because they are no longer under the law. Paul's distinction between being under the law and being under Christ negates the possibility of the law serving as a restriction. Nevertheless, Paul seems to expect the Christian community to respect the law (Rom. 8:4; 7:12; 8:4; 1 Cor. 7:19).

When Paul calls the Torah a *paidegogos,* he treats Torah observance as a boundary marker in terms of it negative function; it restricts actions to prevent one from stepping over the bounds of what is permissible.[16] The works of the flesh that Paul lists in Gal. 5:19–21—fornication, impurity, licentiousness, idolatry, sorcery, etc.—tend to be things the Torah as well as the Greco-Roman morality codes sought to prevent, and against which *halakah* tried to legislate.[17] Because the law no longer has the capacity to create a social reality, it also no longer functions as the means of penalizing violators, and it no longer has the power of a *paidegogos*. The Christian is no longer under its curse. That is, the Torah can no longer serve as the means of punishing offenses. Consequently, Paul treats such things as anathema to the life in Christ rather than as acts that are atoned for within the new covenanted community. If one does them, one does not inherit the kingdom of God (Gal. 5:21). One returns to the jurisdiction of one's former condition, not because Judaism (or, for that matter, the pagan world) sanctioned such things, but because Judaism and paganism are social realities equipped to punish such things.[18] For Paul, the behavioral norms reflected in the Gal. 5:19–21 list

---

[16] See James D. G. Dunn, *The Theology of Paul the Apostle* (Grand Rapids: W. B. Eerdman's, 1998), 346–54. According to Henri Lefebvre, "it transports and maintains specific social relations, dissolves others and stands opposed to yet others" (*The Production of Space,* trans. Donald Nicholson-Smith [Oxford: Basil Blackwell, 1991], 50).

[17] As E. P. Sanders observes, not all of these prohibitions are biblical or Jewish. "Nevertheless, the Jewish content of Paul's ethical views is striking and noteworthy" (*Paul, the Law, and the Jewish People* [Philadelphia: Fortress Press, 1983], 96).

[18] Contra Gordon D. Fee, "Freedom and the Life of Obedience (Galatians 5:1–6:18)" *Review and Expositor,* 91 (spring 1994): 208–209. For example, Ramsay MacMullen's survey of Roman associations, *Roman Social Relations 50 B.C. to A.D. 284* (New Haven: Yale University Press, 1974), cited in Wendell Lee Willis, *Idol Meat in Corinth: The Pauline Argument in 1 Corinthians 8 and 10* (Chico, Calif.: Scholars Press, 1985), 55, provides many examples of how voluntary associations maintained discipline in table fellowship. See Varro *De Re Rustica* 3.2.16 for a discussion of proper decorum. See *Corpus Inscriptionum*

of things to avoid represent the moral order of the old creation that continues to be operative. If an aspect of Paul's ethic could be called interim, this would be it.

Paul characterizes Christianity as a sacred space free of a boundary insofar as acts of charity require no limitation, no restrictions, to prevent one from crossing over into impermissible behavior. Consequently, what Paul calls the fruit of the Spirit, such things as love and generosity (Gal. 5:22–23), forms the moral order of the new creation. We should note that Paul may again be dependent on a tradition in *halakah* that permits the distinction between acts to be limited and acts without limit. Mishnah Tractate *Pe'a* begins with a similar sentiment: "These are the things which have no fixed measure, the corners of the field, and the first-fruits, and the Three Festival offerings, …charity, and the study of Torah. These are the things the fruits of which a man enjoys in this world, and the stock of which remains for him in the world to come, honoring one's father and mother, and charity, and making peace between man and his fellow; but the study of the Torah is equal to them all" (*m. Pe'a* 1.1).

The description of the fruit of the Spirit, the hallmarks of the Christian community, as markers without limit makes sense given the sacred geography of the new creation that does not admit dichotomy. There is no boundary that one crosses where love of neighbor becomes love of the stranger. Only by returning to their original religious observances or by being circumcised can the Galatians identify Paul as their enemy (Gal. 4:16).

Insofar as it is possible to transgress by doing the works of the flesh that are subject to the law, Paul continues to treat the Torah as a border, but he does not refer to the ritual system of Judaism as the means by which the offender restores himself or herself to the community of true worship. In Gal. 6:1–2, the community restores the transgressor through the spirit of gentleness. The realm of Christian activity moves to embrace the offender.

Fortunately, our religious identity does not rely solely on unplotable borders. The marks of the church include baptism, the rite of passage by which one enters into the holiness of the community through the symbolic death that allows us to partake in the Lord's Supper. The

---

Latinarium 14.2112, for a description of the penalty of 4 sesterces for causing a disturbance at table and 12 sesterces for insulting a member of the fellowship. See P. Michigan 5.243 for a list of fines for failure to attend meetings, for taking another's seat, and for other infractions of decorum.

problem is that we do not really die and that we do abide in the flesh, so the temptations of the flesh persist. It is also problematic that there is no physical sign, no physical mark. This absence of physical markers that are so normative for social space in general, and for the social space of the sign system that we inherit from the Old Testament in particular, has gravity. Paul is constantly pulled toward it. If circumcision doesn't matter, then he wishes that those who insist on it would castrate themselves and no longer be circumcised, no longer be ritually pure (Gal. 5:12). If no food is impure, Paul seeks out an image of food that is: "If you bite and devour each other, take care that you are not consumed by one another" (Gal. 5:15). While baptism leaves no physical mark, Paul ends with the proof of his loyalty to Christ by pointing to the marks on his body (Gal. 6:17).[19] This gravity endangers the limitless and eschatological hallmark of charity by pulling the church toward the restrictive force of fixed measures such as moral purity.

I preface my conclusion with what I take to be a description of Christians, provided by R. Elazar of Modim and preserved in the Mishnah. I would have us disassociate ourselves from this description in one respect. "R. Elazar of Modim said, If one profane sacred things, and despise the Holydays, and put his fellowman to shame publicly, and make void the covenant of Abraham our father...and cause the Law to bear a meaning other than in accordance with traditional law, then even though the knowledge of the Law and good deeds are his, he has no share in the world to come (*m. Abot* 3.11).[20]

By our judgment of the other, in this case the Jew, we have more than put our neighbor to shame and have failed to make manifest the fruit of the Spirit. In order for the church to attend to moral purity, we are forced to acknowledge that moral purity is the boundary of other communities. The morality of the Torah—a morality grounded in God's particular will rather than a universal norm—continues to be a guideline for the moral teaching of the church, but its role is subordinate to the desires of the Spirit. If its fulfillment is not a fulfillment of the

---

[19] William Klassen, "Galatians 6:17," *Expository Times* 81 (1970): 378, sees this as a reference to the scars that Paul obtained while pursuing the work of the church. I suspect that Paul's reference is to the life-threatening nature of the wounds, and therefore the use of the word *mark* is symbolically loaded.

[20] While I do not ascribe historical accuracy to mishnaic attributions, my reader might be interested to know that R. Elazar was a contemporary of Jochanan B. Zakkai and was executed by his nephew Bar-Cochba for treachery.

commandment to love our neighbor, then its fulfillment is not a fruit of the Spirit and therefore not a mark of the true church. The mark that makes the church visible is the movable marker, the extension of our activity into the realm of the other as neighbor rather than enemy. The boundary of the church is, as Paul Ricoeur puts it, a horizon toward which we look.[21]

---

[21] Paul Ricoeur, *The Symbolism of Evil*, trans. Emerson Buchanan (Boston: Beacon Press, 1967), 45.

4

Faithfulness and Unity in Romans

Jacob W. Elias

Paul's letters are typically addressed to the church (1 Thess. 1:1; 2 Thess. 1:1; 1 Cor. 1:2; 2 Cor. 1:1) or churches (Gal. 1:2) located in a city or region. Even the deeply personal letter to Philemon names two other individuals and "the church in your house" (Philem. 2). Romans is different. In the opening salutation of this epistle, Paul addresses "all God's beloved in Rome, who are called to be saints" (Rom. 1:7). Not until the close of the letter does Paul utilize the word *ecclesia,* church, and even there only once as a designation for one of the letter's recipient groups: the church that meets in the home of Prisca and Aquila (16:5). Elsewhere in Romans 16 the term *ecclesia* serves to locate Phoebe, the bearer of the letter, as minister in the church in Cenchreae (16:1) and Gaius as a host to Paul and "to the whole church" (16:23). In 16:16b, Paul also speaks representatively for the church as a collection of congregations when he extends a generalized greeting: "All the churches of Christ greet you."

Given Paul's apparent reluctance in Romans to use the word *ecclesia*, one might question whether an examination of this letter will be fruitful for conversations about ecclesiology. It is worth noting that several other Pauline letters also do not employ the word *ecclesia* in the salutation, preferring the designation *saints:* Phil. 1:1; Col. 1:2; Eph. 1:1; cf. also the enlarged reference to saints in the Corinthian letters: 1 Cor. 1:2; 2 Cor. 1:1. Yet in the body of his letters to the Philippians, Colossians, and Ephesians, unlike Romans, Paul makes significant allusions to the *ecclesia*, referring primarily to a universal entity (especially in Ephesians), though sometimes also to the local congregation (Phil. 4:15; Col. 4:16).

Whatever his reasons for avoiding the word *church* in the body of his letter to the Romans, it is readily apparent that Paul has an ecclesiological agenda. His hermeneutic is heavily oriented toward church issues, and his commitment to Scripture when dealing with congregational realities is everywhere evident in Romans. Yet Paul also draws on his own experience as a Pharisee who encountered the risen and crucified Christ on the Damascus road. Under the guidance of the Holy Spirit, Paul draws on Scripture and on his Christophany as he articulates his pastoral theology. And this theology begins not with the concern to clarify soteriology but rather with the intention to speak to ecclesiology. Paul writes Romans having in mind the ethnic, social, cultural, and political realities of the Christian community in Rome.

To understand Paul's ecclesiological concerns in Romans, it may be helpful briefly to reconstruct the history of the Jewish presence in Rome and the emergence of Christian communities there.[1] Some Jews had been living in Rome before 62 B.C.E., but the Jewish population in the city increased dramatically in that year, when the Roman general Pompey settled Judean prisoners of war there. Later many of these freedmen and freedwomen chose to stay in Rome. They established several synagogues, which were diverse and only loosely connected with each other. Gentiles (both Romans and Greek-speaking people from all over the Mediterranean world) also found their way into the synagogues, but apparently most of these Gentiles did not convert to Judaism. They came to be called God-fearers.

The messianic Jewish movement that emerged in Judea and Galilee following the crucifixion of Jesus of Nazareth in about 30 C.E. also spread to Rome during the 30s, 40s and 50s, through artisans and merchants and others (such as Priscilla and Aquila). They traveled to Rome on business and shared the gospel in the synagogues and among acquaintances and with people with whom they made contact in their business dealings.

Conflict within the Jewish community in Rome led Emperor Claudius Caesar to expel Jewish leaders from the city in 49 C.E., and to forbid assembly in the synagogues. Suetonius's history of Claudius Caesar indicates: "Since the Jews constantly made disturbances at the instigation of Chrestus, he expelled them from Rome." Likely this points to disagreement among Roman Jews about whether Jesus was the Messiah. With many of the Jews gone, the gatherings of people who confessed Christ became predominantly Gentile. These groups by

---

[1] Adapted from Wolfgang Wiefel, "The Jewish Community in Ancient Rome and the Origins of Roman Christianity," and Peter Lampe, "The Roman Christians of Romans 16," in *The Romans Debate,* ed. Karl P. Donfried (Peabody, Mass.: Hendrickson Publishers, 1991), 85–101, 216–30.

necessity met with new (Gentile) leadership, and in homes, since synagogues were no longer available to them.

In 54 C.E., when Claudius died, Emperor Nero repealed the expulsion edict, and many of the deported Jews (including Priscilla and Aquila) returned to Rome, finding themselves to be a minority group within congregational life that was largely severed from the synagogues in Rome. Ethnic conflict then erupted between Jews and Gentiles, and theological diversity surfaced. As apostle to the Gentiles, Paul felt called to push on with an evangelistic mission to Spain, and he longed for a solid missionary base in the church in Rome. In the meantime he wanted to complete the project of collecting relief from predominantly Gentile churches for the saints (mainly Jewish believers) in Jerusalem. In about 56 C.E. Paul wrote Romans to introduce himself, articulate his understanding of the gospel, and solicit their support for the expanding mission.

ADDRESSING ETHNIC DIVERSITY IN ROME

The way Paul frames his initial address to his audience in Rome (1:1–7) hints at his ecclesiological agenda in this letter. In Rom. 1:1–6, Paul crafts a self-introduction, in which he presents himself and announces his gospel. Through Jesus Christ he has received "grace and apostleship to bring about the obedience of faith among all the Gentiles" (1:5). Having emphasized the inclusive nature of this vision ("among all the Gentiles"), Paul specifically draws in his Roman hearers: "including yourselves who are called to belong to Jesus Christ" (1:6). The identification of his addressees in 1:7a then seems again to emphasize the broad scope of the gospel vision, this time in traditional Jewish terms: "to all God's beloved in Rome, who are called to be saints." Jews may have heard echoes of scriptural ascriptions of God's historic people as beloved (for example, Ps. 60:5; 108:6) and as saints, set apart and holy (Ps. 16:3; 34:9). Already in the opening of his letter, therefore, Paul seems intent on addressing a particular social reality, namely, Gentile and Jewish believers in Rome together called to be saints who belong to Christ.

Jesus Christ himself is described both in distinctively Jewish terms as "descended from David" and in more Hellenistic categories as the one "declared to be Son of God with power" (1:3–4). The Pauline salutation takes on particular significance, since it combines traditional Hellenistic and Jewish greetings: "Grace to you and peace" (1:7b). It also identifies the source of grace and peace as both "God our Father" (reminiscent of scriptural claims concerning God's special relationship to Israel) and "the Lord Jesus Christ" (now exalted as God's Son in power).

Even in the letter's opening salutation, therefore, Paul clearly has in mind relationships between Jews and Gentiles (later amplified and clarified as relationships between the weak and the strong) within the corporate Christian community in the capital of the empire. Paul writes what we call Romans both to introduce himself and his mission and to enlist the prayerful support of these communities of faith, which had emerged independently of his own missionary efforts. Some of these believers are Jews who were recently allowed to return to Rome after having been expelled by Claudius Caesar for disturbing the peace. Some like Prisca and Aquila (16:3–4) are also known to us from the story in Acts (18:2–3). But more are Gentiles, with lyrical names like Tryphaena and Tryphosa (Rom. 16:12).

Paul's closing (15:14–16:27) confirms that his primary concern is to forge a unity rooted in faithfulness among believers in Rome with diverse theological and ethical understandings. In behalf of "the poor among the saints in Jerusalem" (15:26), Paul desires to complete his collection project among predominantly Gentile churches. Paul views this love gift as a witness to the mutual relationship of reciprocal blessing in Christ for Jewish and Gentile believers (15:27). As he writes the epistle to the house churches in Rome, Paul envisions a missionary thrust to Spain, a new initiative for which he needs a support base in Rome (15:24, 32). But before going to Rome on his way to Spain, Paul anticipates a journey to Jerusalem. He wants to deliver the offering for the Jerusalem saints, a gift of love and a gesture of peace and goodwill from the Gentile believers in Galatia and Corinth and Macedonia toward their Jewish sisters and brothers in Christ living in Jerusalem.

In short, Romans is not in the first place a tract outlining how the individual can be saved; it is an articulation of the gospel as a foundation for uniting diverse communities of faith. Paul in Romans crafts a theology on the basis of which ethnically, socially, and theologically diverse communities of faith might be united for the sake of their mission. Moreover, this unity for the sake of mission is rooted in faithfulness. Central to Paul's concern as Jewish apostle to the Gentiles is to elicit among all nations an obedience rooted in faith, "the obedience of faith" (1:5; 16:26).

The epistle to the Romans therefore presents itself as an inspiring and empowering pastoral word to any church or denomination seeking unity and faithfulness for the sake of the ongoing mission of the church in the world.

But what is that pastoral word? Richard B. Hays outlines four different ways theologians may appeal to Scripture for ethical guidance: rules, principles, paradigms, and symbolic world.[2] Does Paul lay down the law, issue rules for conduct, or establish guidelines for maintaining communal standards? Or is he concerned to articulate ethical principles (for example, love, freedom, purity, or holiness) that will foster the integrity of the church? Or does Paul provide positive paradigms, stories, or summary accounts of characters who model exemplary conduct, or negative paradigms of characters to be avoided? Or does Paul create a symbolic world, ways to perceive reality and shape a faithful response within the contingent social situations in which the church finds itself?

The way Paul portrays God, especially in the opening rhetoric in Romans 1–11, strongly suggests that Paul's strategy is primarily to construct the symbolic world within which the church is to view its life, its relationships, and its mission. Within this symbolic world Paul also includes paradigms and principles and guidelines for living, but the main energy for his pastoral word to these Roman house churches comes from the big picture, the story of God's still-unfolding reign.

THE GOD OF ISRAEL, THE GOD OF ALL

When Paul deals with the issues of Christian unity and faithfulness, he draws foundationally on the narrative of God's own unity and faithfulness. As an apostle and theologian, Paul provides pastoral care and teaching by means of this letter to disparate house churches in Rome. He does so from within the big story of the one God who enters into covenant with a particular people, a story now reaching a climax in Jesus Christ, a story continuing within the community of those who participate in the way of Christ.

In Paul's articulation of the gospel, "the gospel of God" (1:1) which he as apostle proclaims "to bring about the obedience of faith" (1:5; 16:26), we find a dialectic tension between God's universal intention and God's particular strategy (see Appendix 1, p. 60). The God of all is also the God who called a particular people: the descendants of Abraham and Sarah (4:1–25; 9:6–9), of Isaac and Rebecca (9:10–12), of Jacob and not

---

[2] Richard B. Hays, *The Moral Vision of the New Testament: Community, Cross, New Creation: A Contemporary Introduction to New Testament Ethics* ([San Francisco]: HarperSanFrancisco, 1996), 208–9.

Esau (9:12-13). Yet this God who chose Israel also calls both Jews and Gentiles to change status from "not my people" to "my people" (9:24-25).

Both in judgment and in salvation, this God shows no partiality (2:11); all will be judged on the basis of their deeds (2:6). Yet both in judgment and salvation, God gives priority to the Jews: to "the Jew first and also the Greek" (1:16; 2:9, 10).

Humanity has rejected God, who was made known in creation but not acknowledged as God (1:21). Israel pursued righteousness, then stumbled on the stone laid in Zion (9:31-10:3). How does God respond to humanity's rejection, and to Israel's misstep? With reference to humanity Paul says, "God gave them up...to impurity," "to degrading passions," "to a debased mind and to things that should not be done" (1:24, 26, 28). About Israel Paul notes, "God did not spare the natural branches" (11:21) and "a hardening has come upon part of Israel" (11:25).

God gave them up. But did God give up on humankind? God did not spare the natural branches of the family of God tree (11:19, 21). But has God rejected the people of the covenant? In the face of Jewish exclusivity rooted in insistence on Gentile observance of rituals of the law (2:17-27), Paul asserts, "God is one" (3:30). And Paul adds, God "will justify the circumcised on the ground of faith and the uncircumcised through that same faith" (3:30). Both Jews and Gentiles are just by trust, and in this way the alienation between them has been overcome.

In the face of Gentile arrogance expressed in the sentiment that the Jews have had their chance and they blew it (11:13-32), Paul says, "The gifts and the calling of God are irrevocable" (11:29). And Paul breaks into doxology, "O the depth of the riches and wisdom and knowledge of God!" "To [God] be glory for ever!" (11:33a, 36b).

God gave them up, but God did not give up on humankind. God did not spare even the people of the covenant, but ultimately God did not reject them. Indeed, Paul asserts, God "did not withhold his own Son, but gave him up for all of us" (8:32). And Paul concludes his anguished wrestling with Israel's unbelief in Romans 9-11 by expressing his convictions about God's universal intention and God's particular strategy. Here Paul is speaking especially to the Gentiles (note 11:13) about the Jewish story. And, strikingly, Paul now asserts that God's particular strategy has been reversed: to the Gentiles first, but also to the Jews. However, the outcome is still in line with God's universal intention: "The gifts and the calling of God are irrevocable. Just as you were once disobedient to God but have now received mercy because of their disobedience, so they have now been disobedient in order that, by the mercy shown to you, they too may now receive mercy. For God has imprisoned all in disobedience, so that [God] may be merciful to all" (11:29–32).

According to Paul, therefore, a profound tension exists within the heart of God, the God of all, who is also the covenant God of Israel. This tension gets played out in the ways Jews and Gentiles respectively respond to God's all-embracing mercy and God's faithfulness to promises made to the people of the covenant.

Having emphasized the oneness of God, God's impartiality, God's universal intention toward all humanity, Paul comes face to face with the question raised especially by the Jews: Is God faithful? Can God be trusted?

Having underscored God's faithfulness to the covenant people Israel, the priority of the Jews within God's plan, Paul runs into the question raised mainly by the Gentiles: Is God fair? Where is God's justice?

In Paul's pastoral theology this dilemma is resolved in Jesus Christ and in the people who are in Christ. Jesus Christ is the faithful one (1:16–17; 3:21–26) whose obedience unto death on the cross invites both Jews and Gentiles (also slave and free, women and men) to respond in faith. This response to God's grace initiative in Christ is obedience rooted in faith. And such faith-based obedience is foundationally expressed when believers participate in the way of Jesus in their relationship with each other and in their mission to the world.

IN ACCORD WITH CHRIST JESUS, HARMONY!

What, concretely, are the implications that Paul sees for the situation facing Jewish and Gentile believers in Rome? In Rom. 14:1–15:13 Paul articulates ecclesiological and ethical ramifications of the gospel of God. Here Paul offers admonitions concerning life together. These guidelines function within the framework of God's grace initiative in Christ and the overall vision of God's cosmic reign (see Appendix 2, p. 62).

It is to the members of the Roman house churches, both Gentiles and Jews, both strong and weak, that Paul writes in his opening declaration, "The gospel...is the power of God to everyone who believes" (1:16; my translation). It is to these Gentile and Jewish believers, now further classified as the "strong" and the "weak," that Paul in the grand finale of the body of this letter appeals, "Welcome one another, therefore, just as Christ has welcomed you, for the glory of God" (15:7).

The weak are usually understood to be mainly Jewish Christians seeking to continue obedience to the Jewish ritual observances, such as food laws and festival days and circumcision. The strong are often considered to be mainly Gentile believers, although Paul, a Jew, clearly includes himself within this group. The strong demonstrate a certain level of freedom from the purity laws and the religious rituals they have inherited.

Central to the message of the entire letter, including this finale, is the gospel of Jesus Christ whose faithfulness reveals God's righteousness. This gospel demonstrates that indeed the one God is both just toward all and faithful to the particular people whom God had called. God's righteousness is revealed "from faith toward faith, just as it is written, The righteous shall live by faith" (1:17; my translation). God's justice is revealed "from faith." The reference here is to the faithfulness of Jesus Christ even to death on the cross. Paul in Romans 14 and 15 makes repeated reference, in brief sound bites, to the work of Christ:

We are the Lord's (14:8).
Christ died and lived again (14:9).
Do not let what you eat cause the ruin of one for whom Christ died (14:15).
Christ did not please himself (15:3).
Christ has welcomed you, for the glory of God (15:7).
Christ has become a servant of the circumcised on behalf of the truth of God (15:8).

Paul's prayer for the church in Rome articulates his longing that the members might "live in harmony with one another, in accordance with Christ Jesus" (15:5). The life of the church needs to be shaped in conformity to the character of God as made known in Jesus Christ.

In Romans 14 and 15, Paul also enlarges on the nature of the believers' response to God's grace initiative in Christ. As Paul wrote in his theme declaration, God's justice is revealed "from faith" (namely, Christ's faithfulness) "toward faith" (1:17). The reference here is to human faith and human faithfulness as a response to what God has done in Christ. The character of this responsive faith is spelled out for the ethnic and social circumstances that existed within the Christian community in Rome: "Whatever does not proceed from faith is sin" (14:23b). This faith response involves both individual and congregational choices and commitments. Paul admonishes individual believers:

Don't quibble over opinions (14:1).
Neither condemn nor despise the other (14:3, 4, 10, 13).
Resolve never to put a stumbling block in the way of another (14:13).
Pursue what makes for peace and mutual upbuilding (14:19).
Welcome one another! (15:7).

But Paul also longs for the church as a body to manifest a Christ-like character. This entails "walking in love" (14:15), "mutual upbuilding" (14:19; 15:2), and putting up with each other's failings (15:1). Centrally the church responds to God's grace initiative through worship: honoring God, giving thanks to God, glorifying God (14:6; 15:7). This harmony and unity of diverse people (Gentiles and Jews, strong and weak) is eloquently enjoined in Paul's prayer in 15:5–6: "May the God of steadfastness and encouragement grant you to live in harmony with one another, in accordance with Christ Jesus, so that together you may with one voice glorify the God and Father of our Lord Jesus Christ."

Paul views a future in which Jews and Gentiles, the strong and the weak, worship God together with one voice. When disparate peoples welcome one another, as Christ has welcomed them, their blended voices and their lives united in fellowship and mission redound to the glory of God (15:7).

In 15:8–9, Paul recapitulates the formative salvation-historical event that makes such harmony and unity possible: "For I tell you that Christ has become a servant of the circumcised." The Christ event is portrayed in characteristically Jewish terms (we recall, "to the Jews first"). Paul refers to God's fidelity to promises made to Israel, and elaborates: "Christ has become a servant of the circumcised on behalf of the truth of God in order that he might confirm the promises given to the patriarchs." Yet Paul immediately adds a reminder of the universalizing intention behind God's particular strategy (we recall, "also the Greeks"), since the God of all is just and merciful toward all: "and in order that the Gentiles might glorify God for his mercy." A litany of Scriptures follows (Ps. 18:49; Deut. 32:43 LXX; Ps. 117:1; Isa. 11:10 LXX), each of which accents the Gentiles' joyous praise and hope inspired by their inclusion within God's people on the basis of what God has done in Christ. Strikingly, in Romans 3 Paul emphasized that all, both Jews and Gentiles, are under sin, and he underscores that assertion by citing a series of Scriptures (3:9–18). In corresponding fashion, here in the climax of the body of his letter to the Romans (15:7–13), Paul has employed a litany of Scriptures to emphasize the unity of Jews and Gentiles in worshiping God!

Paul clearly wants his Roman hearers to hear the big story of God's work among the covenant people, climaxing in Jesus Christ, and through Christ also in behalf of all peoples. God's dynamic reign has the whole world in view! In Romans 14 and 15 Paul alludes to God's grand intention in various ways:

> We will all stand before the judgment seat of God (14:10).
> "Every knee shall bow..., and every tongue shall give praise to God!" (14:11; echo of Isa. 45:23; Jer. 22:24).
> The kingdom of God is not food and drink but righteousness and peace and joy in the Holy Spirit! (14:17).

Paul urges the church to view its life and relationships from within this cosmic perspective of God's grand intention. Likely that is what Paul has in mind when he urges, "Do not let your good be spoken of as evil" (14:16). What is "your good"? Paul explains in terms of God's reign, the kingdom of God. The expression *your good* goes way beyond any cherished notion of Christian freedom as held by the strong, or a conservative view of tradition as treasure needing to be perpetuated as held by the weak. God's still-unfolding reign is characterized by "righteousness and peace and joy in the Holy Spirit," rather than by prescribed practices ("food and drink"). God's intention for all peoples is glimpsed in the life and mission of the church. And God's mission for the whole world is a good that can easily be maligned as evil when outsiders view the church torn apart in disputes over opinions and neglecting the weightier matters of justice and peace and joy in the Holy Spirit.

CHRISTIAN UNITY AND FAITHFULNESS

How then might the epistle to the Romans speak to our current quest for clarity about the nature of the church?

We have seen that Paul's motivations in writing this letter centered around his longing for a welcoming spirit between Jews and Gentiles in Rome, and between the predominantly Gentile churches and the Jewish communities of believers in Judea. As he anticipates pushing on to Spain in his missionary effort, the apostle Paul writes several house churches in Rome. Paul writes what we call "Romans" both to introduce himself and his mission and to enlist the prayerful support of these communities of faith which had emerged independently of his own missionary efforts.

Our status as twenty-first-century listeners to this first-century letter is brought home to us especially when we struggle to understand what Paul means in Romans 14 and 15 when he refers to the weak and the strong. As twenty-first-century readers of this letter addressed to a first-century audience, we ask, Who are the weak and the strong among us? Who are the weak and the strong within the Mennonite community?

What might be some current, roughly equivalent categories? Should we talk about the conservatives and the liberals among us, those who want to perpetuate traditions from the past and those who assert their freedom from such traditions? Should we talk about such boundary markers as the color of the bumpers on our cars, whether or not we drink wine, how or whether we demonstrate patriotic feelings, how or whether we exercise church discipline?

Regulations concerning kosher and non-kosher foods no longer create divisions in most of the Christian church today. What parallel issues create barriers between us as members of the Mennonite Church and the General Conference Mennonite Church during our process of transformation? How we separate ourselves from the values of the world? Our attitudes and practices and membership understandings with reference to sexuality, especially homosexuality? Our theology and practice in the area of peace/justice making? How we engage in mission in our world?

What might God be saying to us through Paul's letter to the Roman believers? I share a few thoughts.

Christian unity is expressed in our worship, not necessarily in shared opinions about everything. When disputes over opinions pit believer against believer and church against church, we need again and again to glimpse anew the big story of God's still-unfolding reign.

Christian unity also expresses itself in a quest for faithfulness, as enabled by the empowerment of the Spirit. Believers and the community of believers participate in the way of Christ, whose faithfulness unto death on the cross is the prime exemplar of the love that sums up the whole law.

A people seeking to be united and faithful within our culture will inevitably reflect some of God's own anguish, as noted in Scripture. Within God's special calling in Christ, the church as a community of faith has been summoned to a mission that encompasses all. Within God's lavish grace and mercy, all people are invited to acknowledge God and live in harmony with each other. God's character, including the tension between the particular strategy and the universal intention, will be replicated (at least attested) in the character of the community.

What then is the character of the church? Paul does not in the first place lay down the law, or issue a rigid code for maintaining community moral standards. Paul does articulate love as an overarching normative ethical principle, which fosters the integrity of the church. Yet Paul places the law, including love as the fulfillment of the law, within the symbolic world of God's redemptive intervention in Jesus Christ. Jesus' own faithfulness unto death on the cross becomes the paradigm, the model for the community to respond in like faith. Empowered and enabled by God's Spirit, the community of faith participates in the way of Christ. Reflecting the character of God, the church as empowered by the Spirit is both radically welcoming to all and persistently committed to the way of Christ. The church lives within the tension between God's stance of revolutionary inclusion as the one God who is God of all, and God's radically particular strategy as the God of Israel and of Jesus, the God whose justice is climactically revealed in the sacrificial obedience and faithfulness of Jesus Christ.

APPENDIX 1: GOD OF ALL, GOD OF ISRAEL

The one God of all	The God of Israel
God is creator of all, knowable in what God has made, so they are without excuse (1:18–20).	**God called a particular people,** the descendants of Abraham and Sarah (4:1–25), of Isaac and Rebecca, of Jacob and not Esau (9:6–18).
Humanity has rejected God. They knew God, yet they did not honor God nor give God thanks (1:21). They exchanged glory, truth, natural relations (1:23, 25, 26). So God gave them up (1:24, 26, 28).	**Israel stumbled.** Israel pursued righteousness, but stumbled on the stone (9:31–10:3). A hardening has come upon part of Israel (11:25). God did not spare the natural branches (11:21).
In judgment God shows no partiality: God will repay according to each one's deeds. It is not the hearers of the law who are righteous in God's sight, but the doers of the law who will be justified. When Gentiles who do not possess the law do instinctively what the law requires, these are a law to themselves (2:5–16). All, both Jews and Gentiles, are under the power of sin (3:9). All have sinned and come short of the glory of God (3:23).	**In judgment** God shows no partiality: There will be anguish and distress for everyone who does evil, the Jew first and also the Greek, but glory and honor and peace for everyone who does good, the Jew first and also the Greek. God will repay according to each one's deeds. It is not the hearers of the law who are righteous in God's sight, but the doers of the law who will be justified (2:5–16).
In the gospel The gospel is the power of God toward salvation to all who believe (1:16).	**In the gospel** The gospel is the power of God toward salvation to all who believe, to the Jew first and also to the Greek (1:16).
A person is a Jew who is one inwardly, and real circumcision is a matter of the heart—it is spiritual and not literal (2:29). Then what advantage has the Jew? Or what is the value of circumcision (3:1)? What then? Are we (Jews) surpassed (by Gentiles) (3:9)?	Will their (the Jews') faithlessness nullify the faithfulness of God (3:3)? If our injustice serves to confirm the justice of God, is God unjust to inflict wrath, to judge the world (3:5, 6)? If through my falsehood God's faithfulness abounds to God's glory, why am I still being condemned as a sinner (3:7)?
The issue raised by this emphasis on the oneness of God: Where is God's faithfulness? Can God be trusted?	**The issue raised by this emphasis on the faithfulness of God: Where is God's justice? Is God fair?**
	Is God the God of the Jews only? Is God not the God of the Gentiles also? Yes, of Gentiles also, **since God is one;** and God will justify the circumcised on the ground of faith and the uncircumcised through that same faith (3:29–30).

> The gifts and the calling of God are irrevocable.
> Just as you (the Gentiles) were once disobedient to God
> but have now received mercy because of their (the Jews') disobedience,
> so they (the Jews) have now been disobedient in order that,
> by the mercy shown to you (the Gentiles),
> they (the Jews) too may now receive mercy.
> For God has imprisoned all in disobedience,
> so that God may be merciful to all (11:29–32).

APPENDIX 2: THE WEAK AND THE STRONG (ROM. 14:1–15:13)

Characteristics of the weak	Characteristics of the strong
• Eat only vegetables (14:2) • Judge one day better than the other (14:5) • Think "it is unclean" (14:14) • Avoid meat and wine (14:21)	• Believe in eating anything (14:2) • Judge all days to be alike (14:5) • Know that nothing is unclean in itself (14:14); everything is clean (14:20) • Accept meat and wine (14:21)

Admonitions addressed to the weak	Admonitions addressed to the strong	Theological basis for the admonitions
	Welcome those who are weak in faith but not for quarrels over opinions (14:1).	
Don't pass judgment on those who eat (14:3).	Don't despise those who abstain (14:3).	God has welcomed them (14:3).
Who are you to pass judgment on servants of another (14:4)?		Before their own Lord they stand or fall. The Lord is able to make them stand (14:4).
Let all be fully convinced in their own minds (14:5).		
Those who observe the day, observe it in honor of the Lord (14:6). Those who abstain, abstain in honor of the Lord (14:6).	Those who eat, eat in honor of the Lord (14:6).	Honor the Lord, give thanks to God (14:6). We do not live/die to ourselves, but to the Lord; to this end Christ died and lived again, so that he might be Lord of both the dead and the living (14:7, 8, 9).
Why judge (14:10)? Let us no longer pass judgment on one another (14:13).	Why despise (14:10)? Resolve never to put a stumbling block or hindrance in the way of another (14:13).	We all stand before the judgment seat of God. Each will be accountable to God (14:10–12).
	Do not let what you eat cause the ruin of one for whom Christ died (14:15). Do not let your good be spoken of as evil (14:16).	If your brother/sister is injured by what you eat, you are no longer walking in love (14:15). For the kingdom of God is righteousness and peace and joy in the Holy Spirit (14:17). One who thus serves Christ is acceptable to God and has human approval (14:18).

Admonitions addressed to the weak	Admonitions addressed to the strong	Theological basis for the admonitions
Let us then pursue what makes for peace and for mutual upbuilding (14:19).		
	Do not, for the sake of food, destroy the work of God (14:20). It is good not to eat meat or drink wine or do anything that makes your brother or sister stumble (14:21).	Everything is clean but it is wrong for you to make others fall by what you eat (14:20).
The faith that you have, have as your own conviction before God (14:22)		for whatever does not proceed from faith is sin (14:23).
	We who are strong ought to put up with the failings of the weak and not to please ourselves (15:1). Each of us must please our neighbor for the good purpose of building up the neighbor (15:2)	for Christ did not please himself, but "The insults of those who insult you have fallen on me" (written in former days for our instruction, so that we might have hope) (15:3–4).
May God grant you to live in harmony with one another, so that together you may with one voice glorify the God and Father of our Lord Jesus Christ (15:5–6)		in accordance with Christ Jesus (15:5).
Welcome one another (15:7)		just as Christ has welcomed you, for the glory of God (15:7). For Christ has become a servant of the circumcised in order to confirm the promises to the patriarchs and in order that the Gentiles might glorify God for his mercy (15:8; cf. 15:9–12).
May the God of hope fill you with all joy and peace in believing, so that you may abound in hope by the power of the Holy Spirit (15:13).		

BIBLIOGRAPHY

Campbell, William S. "The Rule of Faith in Rom. 12:1–15:13: The Obligation of Humble Obedience As the Only Adequate Response to the Mercies of God." In *Pauline Theology, Volume 3: Romans*, edited by David M. Hay and E. Elizabeth Johnson, 259–86. Minneapolis: Fortress Press, 1995.

Cousar, Charles B. *A Theology of the Cross: The Death of Jesus in the Pauline Letters*. Minneapolis: Fortress Press, 1990.

Dunn, James D. G. *Romans 1–8*, Word Biblical Commentary, vol. 38A, and *Romans 9–16*, Word Biblical Commentary, vol. 38B. Dallas: Word Books, 1988.

Hays, Richard B. "Intertextual Echo in Romans." Chap. 2 in *Echoes of Scripture in the Letters of Paul*. New Haven: Yale University Press, 1989.

Hays, Richard B. *The Moral Vision of the New Testament: Community, Cross, New Creation: A Contemporary Introduction to New Testament Ethics*. [San Francisco]: HarperSanFrancisco, 1996.

Johnson, E. Elizabeth. "Romans 9–11: The Faithfulness and Impartiality of God." In *Pauline Theology, Volume 3: Romans*, edited by David M. Hay and E. Elizabeth Johnson, 211–39. Minneapolis: Augsburg Fortress, 1995.

Johnson, Luke Timothy. *Reading Romans: A Literary and Theological Commentary*. New York: Crossroad Publishing Company, 1997.

Walters, James C. *Ethnic Issues in Paul's Letter to the Romans: Changing Self-Definitions in Earliest Roman Christianity*. Valley Forge, Pa.: Trinity Press International, 1993.

Wire, Antoinette Clark. "'Since God Is One': Rhetoric As Theology and History in Paul's Romans." In *The New Literary Criticism and the New Testament*, ed. Elizabeth Struthers Malbon and Edgar V. McKnight, 210–27. Sheffield, England: Sheffield Academic Press, 1994.

Wright, N. T. "Romans and the Theology of Paul." In *Pauline Theology, Volume 3: Romans*, edited by David M. Hay and E. Elizabeth Johnson, 30–67. Minneapolis: Augsburg Fortress, 1995.

Wright, N. T. *What Saint Paul Really Said: Was Paul of Tarsus the Real Founder of Christianity?* Grand Rapids: W. B. Eerdmans, 1997.

5

Sola Scriptura/*No Other Foundation* and Other Authoritative Sources?

Ben C. Ollenburger

PREFACE

Anabaptists, if I may generalize about the forebears of Mennonites, committed themselves to the restitution of the church. They sought the restitution, not of a church without spot or wrinkle, but of the apostolic church. As Neal Blough says, for these Anabaptists *sola scriptura* constituted the anchorage point, the criterion for what could count as apostolic and could thus function in the critical assessment of church practices, and especially of practices they judged to be corrupt.[1] The term *sola scriptura* has its origin outside Anabaptist or Mennonite circles, of course, in Lutheran ones. Blough's use of it to describe Anabaptists, which has precedent, may justify its appearance in the title of an essay devoted to Mennonite ecclesiology.[2]

Our own tradition has not been noted for preserving Latin slogans. I know of only one, *furor Mennoniticus*, a term coined by the early twentieth-century historian of Mennonites in Russia, Peter Martin

---

[1] Neal Blough, "The Anabaptist Idea of the Restitution of the Early Church" (paper presented to the Anabaptist-Catholic dialogue, Strasbourg, France, October 1999), 8–9. I am grateful to my colleague Walter Sawatsky for providing me with a copy of Blough's essay.

[2] Clarence Bauman concluded that "Formally, the Anabaptists were in complete agreement with the principle of *sola scriptura*." He claimed, as have many others, that the Anabaptists were simply more radical in their application of Scripture's authority, which they extended more broadly (*Gewaltlosigkeit im Täuftertum: Eine Untersuchung zur theologischen Ethik des Oberdeutschen Täufertums der Reformationszeit*, Studies in the History of Christian Thought, vol. 3 [Leiden: E. J. Brill, 1968], 148–49). Timothy George helpfully summarizes Luther's and Menno's (as well as Zwingli's and Calvin's) views of Scripture, in *Theology of the Reformers* (Nashville: Broadman Press, 1988), 79–95, 272–80.

Friesen. By *furor Mennoniticus* he meant the fevered inclination of Mennonites to divide from each other over matters ranging from the profound to the trivial.[3] More familiar to us is "No other foundation," the second part of my title, which abbreviates Menno Simons's motto. Menno quotes 1 Cor. 3:11: "For no other foundation can anyone lay than that which is laid, which is Jesus Christ" (RSV). In context, Paul is reprimanding the Corinthians for the jealous quarreling (the *furor Corinthiorum*?) that has divided them into fractious parties honoring different leaders, or servants (3:3–10). Any such servant, Paul insists, can properly build only on the one foundation, Jesus Christ. At first glance, and perhaps also under careful examination, Menno's motto commends theological criticism of the Anabaptist frenzy for division. But it suggests as well rigorous theological assessment of any union—of the infrastructure of integration—to determine whether its foundation is, indeed and only, Jesus Christ. I will argue that *sola scriptura* adequately names the parameters of such assessment. But I believe that our considerations should begin elsewhere.

THE KERYGMATIC AUTHORITY OF SCRIPTURE

Sola scriptura is understood, and for good reason, as a slogan promoting the singular authority of Scripture. But authority is a complex notion, and especially so in relation to Scripture. This is due in part to the diversity of the church's life, and thus the variety of contexts, and hence the variety of ways in which and purposes for which, the church uses Scripture. Yet the church confesses that every dimension of its diverse life, including its polity, lies within the circumference of Scripture's authority.[4]

Typically, discussions of Scripture's authority focus on its authority for theology and ethics. In these cases, we use Scripture, as David Kelsey

---

[3] Peter M. Friesen, *The Mennonite Brotherhood in Russia, 1789–1910* (Fresno, Calif.: Board of Christian Literature, General Conference of Mennonite Brethren Churches; Hillsboro, Kans.: Mennonite Brethren Publishing House, 1978), 571. Originally published as *Alt-Evangelische Mennonitsche Brüderschaft in Russland, 1789–1910* (1910).

[4] *Confession of Faith in a Mennonite Perspective* (Scottdale, Pa.: Herald Press, 1995) specifically mentions church polity in Article 4, "Scripture," commentary #4, p. 24.

puts it, to authorize theological judgments and moral ones.[5] But, as Kelsey recognizes, Scripture's authority for theology derives from its "authority for the life of the church generally."[6] I would like to be more specific about the way Scripture is authoritative for the church. I propose to understand the church's life—to understand the church, in fact, and especially the congregation—as consisting in a set of practices.[7] On my reading of it, the Mennonite Board of Congregational Ministries document *Growing into Christ* does so as well. It arranges these practices within three arenas: worship, community, and mission.[8] Each of these arenas includes practices constitutive of the church, but I would argue that those included in the first arena, worship, are foundational in and to the others. A church that does not include community (as the document broadly defines it) and mission will be faithless, but a community that does not include worship will be something other than a church. As I have suggested, such practices as community and mission comprise have their foundation in worship: in the church's praise, prayer, and proclamation. To such practices as these Scripture is ingredient. That is, the reading of Scripture is partially constitutive of those practices themselves. For example, we do not read Scripture just to learn about the Lord's Supper, or even to learn how to do it right, but precisely as part of celebrating the Lord's Supper. The uses of Scripture in these practices I shall call *kerygmatic*. They are kerygmatic uses because in them the Christian community takes itself to be addressed by God. In response, the church uses Scripture in its own address to God, so that Scripture

---

[5] David H. Kelsey, *The Uses of Scripture in Recent Theology* (Philadelphia: Fortress Press, 1975).

[6] Ibid., 97.

[7] Elsewhere, Kelsey himself understands the congregation as a set of practices (David H. Kelsey, *To Understand God More Truly: What's Theological about a Theological School* [Louisville: Westminster/John Knox Press, 1992], 200).

[8] *Growing into Christ: An Educational Vision* (Elkhart, Ind.: Mennonite Board of Congregational Ministries, 1987), 2. An earlier document, Ross Thomas Bender, ed., *The People of God: Report of the Study Project to Develop a Model for Theological Education in the Free Church Tradition* (Scottdale, Pa.: Herald Press, 1971), 167–71, similarly stresses practices; its six (discernment, ministry, worship, witness, discipline, universality) could be incorporated, by pairs, into *Growing into Christ*'s three.

forms part of the church's colloquium with God.⁹ In this regard, Mary Ann Tolbert describes Scripture as, for Protestants, "the primary medium of communion with God."¹⁰

We may conceive of Scripture's kerygmatic authority, then, as naming an event, and especially the event of God's address to us in our reading of Scripture. In most places, through most of church history, that reading has been both public and oral, and its context has been liturgical, whether the liturgy be highly formal or off-the-wall. Liturgical acts, including the reading of Scripture itself, the singing of hymns, prayers, preaching, and the Lord's Supper, are self-involving and commissive: they are performative, illocutionary acts—speech-acts, whereby we do something by saying or singing or reading something. While she has in view specifically the Nicene Creed, which Mennonites seldom perform, Catherine Pickstock's remarks apply here as well. She says that "The Creed fulfills its ancient catechetical function...as a performative act of faith.... When we say the Creed, we 'confess' our faith, which is to say, we acknowledge, and even more, we praise. The Creedal enactment of doctrinal and cognitive boundaries is deeply embedded in worship, and locates its genesis in doxology."¹¹

Scripture has a foundational place in those acts of worship and doxology. On Christian understanding, it is also the case that, in and

---

⁹ Johannes Fischer, "Behaupten oder Bezeugen? Zum Modus des Wahrheitsanspruchs christlicher Rede von Gott," *Zeitschrift für Theologie und Kirche* 87, no. 2 (1990): 224–44. I have developed these points, with the aid of Fischer, in "We Believe in God...Maker of Heaven and Earth: Metaphor, Scripture, and Theology," *Horizons in Biblical Theology* 12 (December 1990): 64–96. John Calvin and others have described prayer as a colloquium with God (*Institutes of the Christian Religion*, Library of Christian Classics, vol. 20 [Philadelphia: Westminster, 1960], 3.20.4–5).

¹⁰ Mary Ann Tolbert, "Protestant Feminists and the Bible: On the Horns of a Dilemma," in *The Pleasure of Her Text: Feminist Readings of Biblical and Historical Texts*, ed. Alice Bach (Philadelphia: Trinity Press International, 1990), 11. Peter Hoover contrasts *sola scriptura* (which he attributes to Zwingli) with the Anabaptists, who had "community with Christ." His argument in favor of this view draws exclusively on Scripture for support (Peter Hoover, *The Secret of the Strength: What Would the Anabaptists Tell This Generation?* [Shippensburg, Pa.: Benchmark Press, 1998]).

¹¹ Catherine Pickstock, "Asyndeton: Syntax and Insanity. A Study of the Revision of the Nicene Creed," in *The Postmodern God: A Theological Reader*, ed. Graham Ward (Oxford: Blackwell Publishers, 1997), 299.

through these acts and this reading of Scripture, *God* does something.[12] Worship is not only—but, for that very reason, it can and must also be—the work of the people of God.

Here we may better speak of Scripture's capacity than of its authority, at least as that term is usually understood. But we could also understand authority on the basis of its Latin root, *auctor*, which means both "author" and "originator." The KJV captures this sense when it refers, in Hebrews, to Christ as "the author of eternal salvation" (5:9) and to Jesus as "the author and finisher of [our] faith" (12:2). Scripture has its kerygmatic authority in virtue of its capacity, through the Holy Spirit, to set forth the living Christ,[13] and in that way to mediate—to author—the active presence of God.[14] It seems apt, then, to speak of *sola scriptura*, but only if we associate it with "No other foundation." When I speak of *sola scriptura*, then, I also have in mind "No other foundation."

Scripture derives part of its kerygmatic authority from its character and its content: its character as the unfailingly and uniquely adequate witness to the Triune God—to God's identity and history, and thereby to our own—which is also its content.[15] But Scripture has authorial capacity, and the kerygmatic authority deriving from it, not because of any intrinsic properties of its own as a text, but because of the church's

---

[12] Using speech-act theory and contemporary analytic philosophy, Nicholas Wolterstorff advances an extended, nuanced, and bracing argument for the claim that God uses Scripture to speak by appropriating its discourse as God's own (*Divine Discourse: Philosophical Reflections on the Claim That God Speaks* [Cambridge: Cambridge University Press, 1995]). However, since Wolterstorff takes the canonization of Christian Scripture as God's extended, centuries-long but also centuries-old act of appropriation, he reflects only on what God *was* possibly saying, long time past, by means of this appropriated discourse. Neither does it fall within Wolterstorff's purposes to consider what God may be doing, besides speaking, by way of using Scripture.

[13] John P. Burgess, *Why Scripture Matters: Reading the Bible in a Time of Church Conflict* (Louisville: Westminster John Knox Press, 1998), 43.

[14] Kelsey says that, under certain Christian uses, "Scripture helps 'author' Christian identity, evoking, correcting, and nurturing it" (David H. Kelsey, "Biblical Narrative and Theological Anthropology," in *Scriptural Authority and Narrative Imagination*, ed. Garrett Green [Philadelphia: Fortress Press, 1987], 137).

[15] Robert W. Jenson defends the notion that adequacy is as much as we need from the canon of Scripture (*Systematic Theology*, 2 vols. [New York: Oxford University Press, 1997, 1999], 1:28).

use of it and, in the first place, because of the use God would and does make of it in relation to us. Indeed, a venerable tradition has it that, finally, God is the author of Scripture.[16] God's presence in our worship, through those practices that worship comprises, does not reduce to that of a spectator. In and through and by means of these practices, including Scripture-reading practices, God forms us as Christians and as Christian communities.[17] So, to quote Robert Jenson, "The first and foremost doctrine *de scriptura* is…not a proposition *about* Scripture at all. It is rather the liturgical and devotional instruction: Let the Scripture be read, at every opportunity and with care for its actual address to hearers, even if these are only the reader. The churches most faithful to Scripture are not those that legislate the most honorific propositions about Scripture but those that most often and thoughtfully read and hear it."[18]

Supplementing Jenson, Ingolf Dalferth says that Scripture is "*uniquely normative*," because its "use in the Christian Church continuously gives occasion for the Holy Spirit to inspire persons to have faith in Christ, i.e., to accept the truth of the Gospel."[19] And, hence, to practice the gospel, we should hasten to insist.

THE JURIDICAL AUTHORITY OF SCRIPTURE

In the preceding remarks I have proposed to think of the church in terms of practices, foundational among which are those whose uses of Scripture I have called kerygmatic. As I indicated, we typically consider the authority of Scripture in relation to theology and ethics—our use of

---

[16] Thomas Aquinas, *Summa theologiae* 1, q. 1, a. 10. See Lewis Ayres and Stephen E. Fowl, "(Mis)reading the Face of God: The Interpretation of the Bible in the Church," *Theological Studies* 60 (1999): 519–20. Even so, it is theologically important to remember the humanity of Scripture. Mary M. Knutsen offers a specific argument to this effect, in "What is a Lutheran Theology of the Lord's Supper?" *Word and World* 17 (winter 1997): 28–39.

[17] My references to God's presence do not intend to undermine or contradict the promissory character of the gospel, or of Christology, or for that matter, of ecclesiology, especially one that can refer to a church without spot or wrinkle. See James F. Kay, *Christus Praesens: A Reconsideration of Rudolf Bultmann's Christology* (Grand Rapids: W. B. Eerdmans, 1994), 164–70.

[18] Jenson, *Systematic Theology*, 2:273.

[19] "The Stuff of Revelation: Austin Farrer's Doctrine of Inspired Images," in *Hermeneutics, the Bible and Literary Criticism*, ed. Ann Loades and Michael McLain (New York: St. Martin's Press, 1992), 87–88 (Dalferth's italics).

Scripture in making theological and moral, including ecclesiological, judgments. But I have wanted to suggest that Scripture's singular authority is (and should be) most apparent and direct in those practices, think of them as liturgical practices or devotional ones, in which the Word of God or the gospel is heard and read as address. And I want further to suggest, as have many and greater others before me, that theology is itself parasitic on those practices. However, theology remains no less essential, because practices include what Alasdair MacIntyre calls standards of excellence.[20] Such standards are intrinsic to the practices themselves, which they at least partially define. Theology will be essential, then, to the church's identification and articulation of those standards of excellence, and in that way to the continuation, reform, or renewal of the church's practices—which, at least in the case of Christian practices, include both convictions and affections: think again of the Lord's Supper. And theology itself, on that description, amounts to one of the church's own essential practices, even one of its spiritual practices.[21] Theology, including ecclesiology, is at least—it will always be more but it cannot be less than—the church's own self-critical inquiry into and on behalf of its practices and the communal language, convictions, and affections that they depend on and properly evoke.[22]

---

[20] Alasdair C. MacIntyre, *After Virtue: A Study in Moral Theory* (Notre Dame: Notre Dame University Press, 1981), 175. I have exploited MacIntyre's discussion of (social) practices, and David Kelsey's remarks (in *To Understand God*) on the same topic, in "Theory and Practice in Theological Education," in *The Aims and Purposes of Evangelical Theological Education,* ed. Paul Merritt Bassett (Grand Rapids: W. B. Eerdmans, 2000).

[21] I am speaking, of course, only about the kinds of theology that would include themselves within the church's practices. Theology as an academic discipline, area of inquiry, or speculative activity remains free to pursue countless other things, many of them quite interesting and stimulating, some of them worth the church's consideration. I have in mind, for example, Gordon D. Kaufman's *In Face of Mystery: A Constructive Theology* (Cambridge, Mass.: Harvard University Press, 1993).

[22] So Hans W. Frei, in "Barth and Schleiermacher: Divergence and Convergence," in *Barth and Schleiermacher: Beyond the Impasse?* ed. James O. Duke and Robert F. Streetman (Philadelphia: Fortress Press, 1988), 79. John Howard Yoder spoke in this regard of "Agents of Linguistic Self-Consciousness" ("The Hermeneutics of Peoplehood: A Protestant Perspective," in *The Priestly Kingdom: Social Ethics As Gospel* [Notre Dame: University of Notre Dame Press, 1984], 32–33).

In this self-critical inquiry, in its critical self-assessment, the church makes juridical use of Scripture: it ascribes singular juridical authority to Scripture. At the beginning of this essay I referred to Neal Blough's characterization of the Anabaptists taking *sola scriptura* as an apostolic criterion for assessing then current church practices as corrupt. I doubt neither their judgment nor Blough's. Even so, we modern Mennonites, as it seems to me, have tended to think of Scripture's authority—hence of *sola scriptura* and "No other foundation" with it—in a one-sidedly juridical sense, to the neglect of the kergymatic. C. Norman Kraus, for example, reduces Scripture's authority to the "theological information" it provides, while John H. Yoder, in discussing the authority of the canon, "perceives and conceives of Scriptures as documenting the life and the norming process of a particular community."[23] Regardless of their merits with respect to Scripture's juridical use, these understandings of Scripture's authority as information and documentation remain inadequate to its kerygmatic use.

Let me say at once that my distinction between kerygmatic and juridical is heuristic, and that actually separating the kerygmatic from the juridical would be both artificial and deleterious. Indeed, it is principally in and through the church's kerygmatic reading of Scripture, in the whole panoply of events and practices constituting what we may call worship, and in its catechesis, that we are—or should be—formed as people with the capacities, the tact, and the language requisite to our juridical use of Scripture. Further, just those practices partially defining and constituting the church, including its kerygmatic reading of Scripture, will be among the objects of our reflection and assessment, in our juridical use of Scripture. And these will have the aim of maintaining, renewing, or reforming those very practices.[24] In reality, then, these two senses of *sola scriptura*, the kerygmatic and the juridical, retain—or should retain—an intimate and interdependent relation. Even so, the kerygmatic and the juridical represent heuristically distinguishable uses of Scripture.

---

[23] C. Norman Kraus, *God Our Savior: Theology in a Christological Mode* (Scottdale, Pa.: Herald Press, 1991), 61; John H. Yoder, "The Authority of the Canon," in *Essays on Biblical Interpretation: Anabaptist-Mennonite Perspectives,* Text Reader Series, no. 1, ed. Willard M. Swartley (Elkhart, Ind.: Institute of Mennonite Studies, 1984), 276.

[24] I am here drawing on Charles Taylor, "Social Theory As a Practice," in *Philosophy and the Human Sciences,* Philosophical Papers, vol. 2 (Cambridge: Cambridge University Press, 1985), 91–115. I have elaborated on this in "Theory and Practice," 28–32.

Though the terms "kerygmatic" and "juridical" to describe it are my own, I did not invent the distinction. One can observe it already in the second century: compare Ignatius's kerygmatic use of Scripture in his epistles with Irenaeus's juridical use of it "Against Heresies."[25] Johannes Musäus clearly identified the distinction; he wrote, in 1679, that "the authority of Scripture is a 'double capacity: one to judge other writings and teachings;...another to bring about the assent of faith.'"[26] This latter capacity I have associated with the kerygmatic authority of Scripture. Musäus's language here is identifiably Lutheran. We may use it even so, modifying it in the direction of my remarks above, to say that, in worship, God also uses Scripture. The point would be to stress God's initiative, and to associate Scripture's authority as closely as possible with that initiative in Jesus Christ, the foundation other than whom no one can lay. Each of the Reformation traditions, Mennonite included, made this point and grounded Scripture's authority in God's own work. In what follows I will try to relate these considerations to issues of polity, the juridical use of Scripture, and "other sources."

THE CHURCH AS A POLITY FOR READING SCRIPTURE

In his screed against the twin evils of fundamentalism and biblical criticism, Stanley Hauerwas describes the church as "the polity for reading and understanding Scripture."[27] This adroit description helps make sense of the importance of *sola scriptura* in the Reformation, which we may consider a debate about ecclesiology and, hence, polity. More precisely, as regards our discussion here, we may consider it a debate about the right polity for reading and understanding Scripture. Each confessional branch of the Reformation—Lutheran, Reformed,

---

[25] "Against Heresies" is the title of Irenaeus's most often cited work. See David S. Dockery, *Biblical Interpretation Then and Now: Contemporary Hermeneutics in the Light of the Early Church* (Grand Rapids: Baker Book House, 1992) 45–73. Dockery uses the terms "functional" and "authoritative" for the distinction to which I am pointing.

[26] Jenson, *Systematic Theology*, 2:273. I make no claim that the categories "juridical" and "kerygmatic" are exhaustive, or even that they are adequate. Musäus used the terms "inciting" or "productive" for what I have called kerygmatic, and "canonical" or "normative" for what I have called juridical (Jenson, *Systematic Theology*, 1:29, n. 21).

[27] Stanley Hauerwas, *Unleashing the Scripture: Freeing the Bible from Captivity to America* (Nashville: Abingdon Press, 1993), 27.

Anglican, and Mennonite—came to focus this debate soteriologically. Both the Church of England's Thirty-Nine Articles (1563) and the Reformed Westminster Confession (1646) discuss the authority of Scripture in relation to its sufficiency and clarity regarding what is necessary for salvation.[28] Both the Lutheran Augsburg Confession (1530) and the Mennonite Dordrecht Confession (1632) employ a narrative expansion of the Apostle's Creed to anchor Scripture's authority in the biblical story of creation and redemption, and thus in God's initiative and action.[29] Each of these confessions reflects, more or less obviously, a polemic against Roman Catholic doctrine and polity. Naturally, the Dordrecht Confession goes on to express significant differences from both Reformed and Lutheran polities.[30] The question, then, is not whether the church is the polity for reading and understanding Scripture, but rather what polity does or should the church embody? More fundamentally, how does the church go about trying to answer that question?

Sola scriptura may stand as an answer to both questions. That is, regarding the question, "How shall the church determine its polity?" *sola scriptura* may answer, "In consonance with Scripture."[31] And regarding the contingent and contested question, "What polity should the church embody?," *sola scriptura* may answer that it will be a polity in which

---

[28] The Thirty-Nine Articles, Article 6; The Westminster Confession, Article 1.7.

[29] Augsburg cites the creed in Article 3, on the work of Christ, while Dordrecht merely quotes it without attribution in Article 4, which addresses the same subject. Incidentally, Dordrecht prefaces its quotation of the creed with "We believe and confess on the authority of Scripture." The soteriological priority of Scripture's authority remains in the *Confession of Faith in a Mennonite Perspective* (1995), which confesses that "Through the Holy Spirit, God moved human witnesses to write what is needed for salvation" (Article 4, paragraph 2).

[30] For example, Augsburg has articles on justification and the office of ministry following immediately those on the fall and redemption (Articles 2–5), while Dordrecht places articles on the law of Christ, repentance, and baptism between its articles on God the creator, redemption, and the church, and only then speaks of church offices (Articles 1–9).

[31] "As participants in the church's teaching ministry and as theological educators, we believe that faithful belief and practice is to be measured above all by consonance with Scripture" (*Ministerial Formation and Theological Education in Mennonite Perspective* [Elkhart, Ind.: Associated Mennonite Biblical Seminaries, 1992], 6). Marlin Miller was the principal author of this statement.

parties to debates on all such matters must refer themselves to Scripture as their singularly indispensable common ground.[32] Of course, these answers remain formal. They do not address, for example, questions of how Scripture will be read, what will count as "consonance with Scripture," or who will be permitted to participate in its reading. *Sola scriptura* was, after all, the formal principle of the Lutheran Reformation, whose material principle was justification by faith, including both *sola gratia* and *sola fide*—by grace alone through faith alone. As it funds the dialectic of law and gospel, this material principle issues in a hermeneutical guide for the interpretation of Scripture. And when the Augsburg Confession places its article on the office of the ministry immediately following the article on justification and prior to an article on the church, it suggests a privilege regarding, if not a limitation on, who will count as an interpreter. Its Article 28, in a section on "Disputed Matters," further limits a decisive part of that privilege, and hence authority, to bishops.

A Mennonite polity deriving from Dordrecht would differ in important respects from a Lutheran one. However, the two confessional traditions preserve a similar and significant caveat. Augsburg, while requiring parish ministers and churches to obey their bishops, cancels this requirement in case the bishops "teach, introduce, or institute anything contrary to the Gospel" (Article 28). And the Mennonite Ris Confession (1766/1895), in its Article 24, on the ministry, while requiring respect and honor for the ministerial offices and those who hold them, stipulates that this "not be in any wise binding upon the conscience except insofar as their words and management are in accord with the Word of God."[33]

In other words, the confessional statements of both traditions strongly imply a polity according to which the gospel or the Word of God serves as a criterion for assessing putative expressions of it—putative expressions of the gospel or the Word of God—put forward by

---

[32] "There is no teaching office in the church that can give a decisive answer to any question of faith and morals which does not ground its teaching in the common norm of all Christianity, and that is conveyed by Scripture alone" (Carl E. Braaten, *Principles of Lutheran Theology* [Philadelphia: Fortress Press, 1983], 24).

[33] Howard John Loewen, *One Lord, One Church, One Hope, and One God: Mennonite Confessions of Faith*, Text Reader Series, no. 2 (Elkhart, Ind.: Institute of Mennonite Studies, 1985), 97.

those ordained to do so. In the respective traditions, of course, Scripture was the singularly authoritative text to which such critical assessments had to refer. It follows ineluctably that putative expressions of the gospel or of the Word of God had to be construed as interpretations of Scripture, whatever else they may be. And since these interpretations had to be assessed with reference to Scripture, a distinction between text and interpretation follows just as ineluctably. Indeed, Gerhard Ebeling identified the preservation of just this distinction, between text and interpretation, as fulfilling one of the essential functions of *sola scriptura*.[34]

Hauerwas, after quoting Ebeling at length, concludes that, when it "is used to underwrite the distinction between text and interpretation," *sola scriptura* is heresy. Hauerwas bases this condemnation on his own assumption that the distinction itself "assumes that the text of the Scripture makes sense separate from a Church that gives it sense."[35] It need assume no such thing. Hauerwas does well to resist the separation of text and interpretation (try to think of an uninterpreted text). And he is certainly right to insist on the conjunction of church and canon, since the biblical narrative and the community—the church—are, both and together, "initiated by God."[36] Without the canon, there can be no

---

[34] Gerhard Ebeling, *The Word of God and Tradition: Historical Studies Interpreting the Divisions of Christianity* (Philadelphia: Fortress Press, 1968), 136.

[35] Hauerwas, *Unleashing Scripture*, 27. Hauerwas is here the source of my reference to Ebeling. See also Ebeling's remarks in "'Sola Scriptura' und das Problem der Tradition," in *Das Neue Testament als Kanon*, ed. Ernst Käsemann (Göttingen: Vandenhoeck & Ruprecht, 1970), 282–335; A. H. J. Gunneweg, "Sola Scriptura," *Beiträge zu Exegese und Hermeneutik des Alten Testaments*, vol. 1 of *Sola Scriptura* (Göttingen: Vandenhoeck & Ruprecht, 1983), 185–98.

[36] John Sykes, "Narrative Accounts of Biblical Authority: The Need for a Doctrine of Revelation," *Modern Theology* 5 (1989): 332. Insofar as Hauerwas suggests that the church (and tradition) were realities "prior" to Scripture, he is mistaken (see Hauerwas, *Unleashing Scripture*, 24, where he is summarizing Georges Florovsky). In a theologically important sense, Scripture was prior even to Jesus of Nazareth, to his herald, John, and to John's father and Jesus' maternal (!) uncle, Zechariah.

church; without the church, there could be no canon.[37] It is in this respect that, in Hauerwas's terms, the church gives Scripture its sense.

That way of putting it remains open to different understandings, which themselves open onto different polities. For example, the church itself may give Scripture its irrevocably normative sense in specific arenas and in definitive instances of interpretation. Pope John Paul II has done so by "the ordinary universal Magisterium" of the Roman Catholic Church on the matter of priestly ordination, and specifically in ruling against the ordination of women to the priesthood. In this polity, the magisterium—the church's authoritative teaching office—"is entrusted with the authentic interpretation of the Word of God."[38] Regarding the ordination of women to the priesthood, Scripture has been assigned its normative sense and need not be consulted further; text and interpretation are collapsed into one. This polity is not open to assessing whether the bishop's pronouncement actually expresses the gospel (Augsburg) or the Word of God (Ris). Of course, the Roman pontiff does not claim the slogan *sola scriptura* as his own, and in the polity that guides him, the Word of God or revelation consists in both Scripture and tradition. Further, since tradition here includes the history of the church's normative interpretation of Scripture, it also includes the magisterium itself, "invested," as Cardinal Ratzinger has put it, "with the authority of Christ."[39]

---

[37] Sykes, "Narrative Accounts," 332. It should be understood that the canon of Scripture is a necessary but not sufficient condition of the church's existence, and vice versa.

[38] Speaking for the Congregation for the Doctrine of the Faith, Joseph Cardinal Ratzinger also describes it as "a Magisterium sacramentally invested with the authority of Christ (cf. *Lumen Gentium*, 21)" ("Letter of October 28, 1995, Regarding the SCDF Responsum on *Ordinatio Sacerdotalis*," available at http://www.newadvent.org/docs/df95lt.htm, accessed 9 August 2000).

[39] Ibid. In Kelsey's terms, the teaching office (or magisterium) constitutes part of the "modality in which the revealed word is present" (Kelsey, *Scripture in Recent Theology*, 97). For a sympathetically critical account of the magisterium's role in biblical interpretation, see Sandra M. Schneiders, *The Revelatory Text: Interpreting the New Testament As Sacred Scripture*, 2nd ed. (Collegeville, Minn.: The Liturgical Press, 1999), 81–86. Cf. Christine E. Gudorf, "Magisterium and the Bible: North American Experience," *The Bible and Its Readers*, Concilium 1991/1, ed. Wim Beuken, Seán Freyne, Anton Weiler (London: SCM Press, 1991), 79–90.

The Reformation, especially in its radical wings, sponsored an alternative polity. Even a century before Luther, at the Council of Constance, the Chancellor of the University of Paris, Jean Gerson, now celebrated as the author of classic spiritual texts, represented a Catholic conciliar polity in the prosecution of the Czech reformer Jan Hus for heresy. In his defense, Hus invoked the "principle of *sola scriptura*"—more precisely, he asked to be instructed "by 'better and more relevant Scripture than those that I have written or taught.'"[40] Gerson contended that this would finally countenance any interpretation at all. Rather, according to Gerson, the proper sense of Scripture, Scripture's authoritative meaning, must be determined in accordance with tradition—determined, that is, in concert with the doctors of the church, especially the early church, insofar as their judgments have received the church's official approbation.[41] Here again, issues of ecclesiology and polity were at the fore. Indeed they were and remain central. According to Cardinal Ratzinger, the decisive ecclesiological problem with Protestants consists less in the independence of God's Word from tradition than in the independence of both from an authoritative office.[42]

In his defense, Hus also appealed to early church doctors and tradition, especially to the same Augustine who was chief among

---

[40] Mark S. Burrows, "Jean Gerson on the 'Traditioned Sense' of Scripture As an Argument for an Ecclesial Hermeneutic," in *Biblical Hermeneutics in Historical Perspective*, ed. Mark S. Burrows and Paul Rorem (Grand Rapids: W. B. Eerdmans, 1991), 162, 166. Burrows advocates for Gerson in his account of the dispute with Hus, contrasting Gerson's traditioned hermeneutics with Hus's appeal to the right of private judgment (ibid., 166). The contrast, thus expressed, is tendentious on its face, and the charge is plainly false as well (see the account of Hus's trial in Matthew Spinka, *John Hus at the Council of Constance* [New York: Columbia University Press, 1965]).

[41] Burrows, "Jean Gerson," 160. This follows from Gerson's strict reliance on Henry Totting of Oyta, whose position on the matter Burrows himself describes (ibid., 158–66).

[42] So Miroslav Volf, *After Our Likeness: The Church As the Image of the Trinity* (Grand Rapids: William B. Eerdmans, 1998), 55. So also Paul R. Hinckley, "The Lutheran Dilemma," *Pro Ecclesia* 8 (1999): 391–422. Volf offers a compelling argument, against Ratzinger (and by extension, Hinckley) for a Free Church ecclesiology. See A. James Reimer's critical evaluation of Volf's argument in this volume.

Gerson's traditional doctors.[43] For his part, Hus included John Wyclif—a heretic whose bones had been unearthed to be burned—among the church's doctors, though he disagreed with Wyclif on many points. Not coincidentally, both Wyclif and Hus produced vernacular translations of Scripture. In other words, the tradition that informed Hus's interpretation of Scripture included a historically embodied principle of ecclesial self-criticism—and criticism of its magisterium—grounded in and on Scripture, to which the people should have access.[44] And it included the concomitant notion that the true church has Christ alone as its head. Here the slogan *sola scriptura* joins "No other foundation," which reverses the metaphorical image from head to foundation, but to the same end. Following his trial at the Council of Constance, Jan Hus was burned at the stake, on 6 July 1415. This civil execution of an ecclesial verdict was in fact the deconstruction of its very premise. A church that kills dissenters, or employs the state to do so, in defense of itself as the church of Jesus Christ, forfeits any presumptive—not to mention exclusive—claim to that very identity.[45]

These two examples, one contemporary and the other now ancient, illustrate the significance of the distinction that Hauerwas calls heretical: the distinction between text and interpretation.[46] Even so, I mean to grant a part of Hauerwas's point. In its foundationally kerygmatic uses of Scripture, in its liturgical and devotional practices, in worship, the church does indeed, both inevitably and properly, collapse text and interpretation. It does so as well in its moral practices, in the church's

---

[43] Burrows, "Jean Gerson," 165. Hus's many references to Augustine are reported in Spinka, *John Hus at the Council of Constance*. While we may count Hus as among the earliest radical reformers, his views on the predestination of the *congregatio fidelium*, derived from Augustine, contrast sharply with subsequent Anabaptist and Mennonite voluntarist emphases.

[44] Volf offers illuminating theological discussion on the point, unrelated to Hus, in *After Our Likeness*, 164–66 and elsewhere.

[45] In a speech in the Czech Republic, on 27 April 1997, Pope John Paul II referred to July 6 as "the anniversary of the tragic death of Jan Hus."

[46] Kathryn Tanner argues for the theological importance of distinguishing between the text's plain sense and any specification or interpretation of it, in Kathryn Tanner, "Theology and the Plain Sense," in *Scriptural Authority and Narrative Interpretation*, ed. Garrett Green (Philadelphia: Fortress Press, 1987), 58–78. Her arguments apply as well to the distinction of text and interpretation, as I have set it out above.

acts and patterns of obedience, including its polity. In each of these dimensions of the church's life, but also and especially in their totality, consistent with its own—consistent with our own—confession, the church is a commentary on Scripture. To employ a different metaphor, in the church Scripture has its social embodiment.[47] In these respects, the church re(-)presents the text. Or it performs the text.

Nicholas Lash has proposed that "the fundamental form of the *Christian* interpretation of Scripture is the life, activity and organization of the believing community."[48] In its diverse life, the church performs Scripture: "Performing the text," as Lash puts it, "enacts the conviction that these texts are most appropriately read as the story of Jesus, the story of everyone else, and the story of God."[49] Lash's suggestion accords with both the narrative shape that Dordrecht gives soteriology and Dordrecht's soteriological grounding of Scripture's authority. As Lash goes on to say: "It follows that, for the practice of Christianity, the performance of the biblical text, to be true, it must be not only 'true to life,' but 'true to *his* life;' and not only 'true to his life,' but 'true to God.' That it is so, and may be made so, is at once our responsibility, our hope and our prayer."[50]

The responsibility of which Lash here speaks requires the church also to make juridical use of Scripture, just in order to assess whether its

---

[47] I have employed both metaphors previously, the first in "Biblical and Systematic Theology: Constructing a Relation," in *So Wide a Sea: Essays on Biblical and Systematic Theology*, Text-Reader Series, no. 4, ed. Ben C. Ollenburger (Elkhart, Ind.: Institute for Mennonite Studies, 1991), 111–45; see further John P. Burgess, *Why Scripture Matters* (Louisville: Westminster John Knox Press, 1998), 120–40; and the second in "We Believe in God." I borrowed the notion of Scripture's social embodiment from Vigen Guroian, "Bible and Ethics: An Ecclesial and Liturgical Interpretation," *Journal of Religious Ethics* 18 (1990): 133–34. He borrowed it, in a somewhat altered form, from Wayne A. Meeks, "A Hermeneutics of Social Embodiment," *Harvard Theological Review* 79 (1986): 177–86.

[48] Nicholas Lash, "Performing the Scriptures," in *Theology on the Way to Emmaus* (London: SCM Press, 1986), 42 (Lash's italics).

[49] John Milbank brings together the notions of performance and practice—and theology as "the explication of practice"—under the metaphor of music ("Postmodern Critical Augustinianism: A Short *Summa* in Forty-two Responses to Unasked Questions," in Ward, *The Postmodern God*, 265–78).

[50] Lash, "Performing the Scriptures," 45.

performance, its commentary, its social embodiment is true: whether it is faithful. On this matter I have already remarked. Here I add only that such assessment, or critical self-assessment, implies and requires a rupture, a disruptive distinction between text and interpretation, on behalf of but thus also and necessarily against the church. This, too, forms part of the meaning of *sola scriptura* and "No other foundation."

OTHER SOURCES?

But can Scripture alone suffice? Must we not make use, authoritative use, of other (re)sources as well? Obviously, Cardinal Ratzinger would insist that we must. But what about Protestants (and Mennonites *are* Protestants)? In 1638, the Anglican scholar William Chillingworth answered that "The Bible, I say, the Bible only is the religion of Protestants!"[51] Professor Chillingworth had a point, but Protestants have always made authoritative use of sources beyond Scripture—they have used additional sources, that is, to authorize theological judgments, in Kelsey's terms. The author of *sola scriptura*, Martin Luther, drew authoritatively on church tradition, especially against our forebears![52] Those same forebears, at Dordrecht and elsewhere, drew authoritatively on the Apostle's Creed. Theologians and confessions, Protestant or otherwise, have appealed to church dogma, a mandated liturgy,[53] the orders of creation, the unmediated testimony of the Holy Spirit, and in various ways to social or personal experience or their analyses, not to mention the putative deliverances of reason. But it would be mistaken, I believe, to gather the objects of these various "drawings on and appealings to" into a single category that stands over against Scripture alone. If by *sola scriptura* we also mean "No other foundation," then we are freed to make constructive and critical use of any resources that enhance our interpretation of Scripture, which is also to say, with Lash,

---

[51] William Chillingworth, *The Religion of Protestants: A Safe Way to Salvation or an Answer to a Book Entitled Mercy and Truth or, Charity Maintain'd by Catholiques, Which Pretends to Prove the Contrary* (Ann Arbor: University Microfilms, 1975).

[52] On Luther's view and use of tradition, see John M. Headley, "The Reformation As Crisis in the Understanding of Tradition," *Archiv für Reformationsgeschichte* 78 (1987): 5–22.

[53] This is Robert Jenson, a Lutheran: "The slogan *sola scriptura*, *if* [Jenson's italics] by that is meant 'apart from creed, teaching office, or authoritative liturgy,' is an oxymoron" (Jenson, *Systematic Theology*, 1:28).

our corporate, ecclesial performance of Scripture, as faithful witness to that foundation, and—hence and necessarily—to the Triune God. By the same token, we have a minimal criterion for assessing the use of such other sources as may be providentially available to us: do they enhance our kerygmatic, juridical, and corporately performative interpretation of Scripture, consistent with "No other foundation?"[54]

One pattern for including theology's other sources may be found in the so-called Wesleyan quadrilateral. While John Wesley never used the term, and neither does the United Methodist Church's *Book of Discipline*, the latter text has given the Wesleyan quadrilateral official status in its definition of "Our Theological Task"—that is, the theological task of the church.[55] The quadrilateral holds that theology must make use of Scripture, tradition, reason, and experience. On one hand, theology cannot avoid using Scripture, for reasons that we need not rehearse. Indeed, the *Book of Discipline* acknowledges the "primacy of Scripture." But it continues immediately to insist that "our attempts to grasp its meaning always involve tradition, experience, and reason."[56] No one should want to deny this. Any interpretation of Scripture will be situated within some tradition, academic or ecclesial or both, regardless of whether we expressly invoke that tradition. Without employing our rational capacities, or reason, we could not even read Scripture, much less converse about our readings. And by now we all recognize that experience, one way or another, in some form or another, bears inevitably on our readings of Scripture.

The quadrilateral does not intend merely to acknowledge certain inevitabilities; rather, it points to indispensable resources that together

---

[54] John Howard Yoder (borrowing from Karl Barth) refers in this regard to "other lights," which can, but need not, amount to "a competitive revelation claim"—one in competition with Jesus (John H. Yoder, "Christ, the Light of the World," in *The Royal Priesthood*, ed. Michael G. Cartwright [Grand Rapids: Eerdmans, 1994], 187–89). See also Gerard Loughlin, "The Basis and Authority of Doctrine," in *The Cambridge Companion to Christian Doctrine*, ed. Colin E. Gunton (Cambridge: Cambridge University Press, 1997), 41–64.

[55] *The Book of Discipline of The United Methodist Church* (Nashville: United Methodist Publishing House, 1996), 74–80.

[56] Ibid., 76. *The Book of Discipline* here speaks of "sources and criteria" of authentic Christian witness. An Episcopal quadrilateral (Chicago-Lambeth, 1886) includes Scripture, creed, sacraments, and the historic episcopacy. But these are "principles" for the unity of the church.

form a dynamic matrix.[57] Even so, there remain important differences among the components of that matrix. Scripture, tradition, reason, and experience are different kinds of things. Scripture is (or is not less than) a particular corpus of texts. Tradition typically does have particular textual expressions, but it will be difficult to achieve consensus, even within a particular tradition, about the extent of these expressions and their relative bearing. Moreover, the larger and more influential part of any tradition surrounds those expressions and is especially embodied in practices, which include Scripture-reading practices. It will not do, then, to collapse Scripture into tradition (or interpretation) with the observation that "Scripture is, after all, part of the tradition."[58] It will not do for two reasons.

First, David Kelsey shows that "the concepts 'tradition' and 'Scripture' are not on a logical par. 'Tradition' is used to name, not something the church uses, but something the church *is*, insofar as her reality lies in a set of events and practices that can be construed as a single activity. 'Scripture' is used to name, not something the church is, but something she must *use*...to preserve her self-identity."[59]

And second, more than self-identity is at stake in the church's use of Scripture. Fidelity, for example. Indeed, part of any church's juridical use of Scripture consists in scrutiny of what that church is, and thus of its tradition(s).[60]

---

[57] For examples, see Kelsey, *Scripture in Recent Theology*, 122–47; Donald W. Dayton uses the term "matrix" in describing the Quadrilateral, in "The Use of Scripture in the Wesleyan Tradition," in *The Use of the Bible in Theology: Evangelical Options,* ed. Robert K. Johnston (Atlanta: John Knox Press, 1984), 129.

[58] Pamela Dickey Young, *Feminist Theology/Christian Theology: In Search of Method* (Minneapolis: Fortress Press, 1990), 71.

[59] Kelsey, *Scripture in Recent Theology*, 96. Compare Kelsey's discussion of Scripture and tradition with that of Sandra Schneiders (chap. 3 in *The Revelatory Text*) and Heiko Oberman (chap. 12 in *The Dawn of the Reformation: Essays in Late Medieval and Early Reformation Thought* [Edinburgh: T. & T. Clark, 1986]). Schneiders partially inverts Oberman's distinctions between "Tradition" and "tradition."

[60] John Howard Yoder, "The Authority of Tradition," in *The Priestly Kingdom*, 69. Walter Kasper, a Roman Catholic theologian and now bishop, says that "interpretation is the condition of tradition," and tradition (even "dogma itself") must "in its turn, be interpreted in the light of Scripture" (*Theology and Church* [New York: Crossroad, 1986], 6).

Any such scrutiny or self-critical assessment, on behalf of the church's fidelity, will involve (one hopes!) the use of reason. It will also refer to and draw on experience. Indeed, reason and experience work together. We identify our experience through the rational activity of bringing it into language under certain concepts that are publicly shared.[61] "An...experience can be identified only under a certain description, and reference must be made to that description in any explanation that is offered."[62] Tradition constitutes a rich resource for such descriptive and explanatory purposes; so, perforce, does Scripture (as I will illustrate below). Wesleyans, and not only they, testify to the experience of justification and sanctification. Of course, experience can be brought to language under other descriptive and explanatory resources—products of reason (and one or another tradition) that proffer their own accounts of the world: psychology, natural sciences, philosophy, history, and countless others. Of these, too, we make occasional, critical, and properly ad hoc use, recognizing that they are not the products of reason alone, since nothing is, but also of corrupt desire, self-deceit, and the will to power—of sin. And we both can and must acknowledge that our tradition has been shaped and changed and challenged by the experience of those who have found it, in various ways and at various times, to be corrupt and oppressive. Reflection on that kind of experience has, from time to time, both reformed and revitalized our reading of Scripture. Corrupt desire, self-deceit, and the will to power accompany this human activity, this churchly practice, too.[63] Identifying, exposing, and repenting of these sins are among the ends intrinsic to both our kerygmatic and our juridical uses of Scripture, for which nothing substitutes. As James McClendon says, "Every practice is

---

[61] As an example, one cannot have the experience of alienation if one lacks the concept *alienation*, though one may be just as miserable, or more so, for lacking it. On these matters see George Lindbeck, *The Nature of Doctrine: Religion and Theology in a Postliberal Age* (Philadelphia: Westminster Press, 1984).

[62] Wayne Proudfoot, *Religious Experience* (Berkeley: University of California Press, 1985), 218.

[63] On the topic see, among others, Mary McClintock Fulkerson, "'Is There a (Non-Sexist) Bible in This Church?' A Feminist Case for the Priority of Interpretive Communities," *Modern Theology* 14 (1998): 225–42.

vulnerable to corruption. This one practice, however, contains its own corrective."[64]

The quadrilateral need not, then, contrast with *sola scriptura*.[65] To be sure, its conjunctive account of theology's, hence of the church's, resources opens a clearer space for the appreciation and refinement of them. In this regard, I suggest that we see *sola scriptura* and the quadrilateral as mutually corrective. The quadrilateral softens the excessively disjunctive mood of *sola scriptura*, while *sola scriptura* guards against any suggestion that tradition, reason, and experience may constitute theological sources and criteria independent of Scripture. The quadrilateral guards against illicit foreclosure on Scripture's interpretation, since tradition, reason, and experience remain—because the church's and everyone's life remains—embedded in history, while *sola scriptura* warns against category mistakes, such as when we may be tempted to speak of the deliverances of reason or of experience. Interpreted from our own tradition, the quadrilateral reinforces convictions that the responsibility and privilege and process of interpretation must never be thought of as closed or completed—that even a church-wide consensus of long standing, even if it is confessionally enshrined and sustained by ecclesial authority, may be renewed or revised or reformed in relation to the interpretation of Scripture.

Finally, the quadrilateral may aid us in granting the importance of what Richard Hooker called Scripture's silence. Hooker, citing Tertullian, wrote that Scripture "uses silence" on matters marginal to the ends and purposes for which God gave it.[66] Of course, discerning those ends and purposes, and whether anything at all is marginal to them, requires the practical reasoning, which is to say the wisdom, of the

---

[64] James Wm. McClendon, *Systematic Theology: Doctrine* (Nashville: Abingdon Press, 1994), 35.

[65] According to Braaten, "*sola scriptura* means that everything essential in the original apostolic preaching which founded the church is written down in Scripture, and that no later tradition can negate or supersede it" (Braaten, *Principles of Lutheran Theology*, 24).

[66] In his *Laws of Ecclesiastical Polity*, II.5.7. I depend here on John Booty, "Richard Hooker and the Holy Scriptures," *SEAD Occasional Paper 3* (May 1995).

righteous (Luke 1:7).[67] Regardless, on different matters we will figure Scripture differently. Scripture may figure heavily and quite directly in considerations of whether to baptize infants or of how to speak of God's action in our salvation, but less heavily and quite indirectly in considerations of how far apart to paint the lines in church parking lots. Of course, we may and should hope that even these kinds of considerations, and all of those that involve us in the juridical use of Scripture, would be shaped—and that the processes guiding such considerations would be shaped—by Scripture, and in particular by its *kergymatic* use. For example, we may hope that such considerations would avoid bitterness and calumny among people committed to different views on how narrowly or how broadly to draw the lines.

A CASE IN POINT

Anabaptists and their Mennonite progeny have been much concerned with drawing, erasing, and re-drawing lines. They and we have written scores of confessions and confessional statements since Schleitheim, in 1527, some of them intended to confirm a division and mark a boundary of exclusion—the *furor Mennoniticus*—and others to facilitate (re)union by articulating common confessional ground. Perhaps the sheer number of Mennonite confessions and the substantial differences among them have contributed to reservations about the kind of authority we should grant any one of them.[68]

Recently, as it seems to me, we have witnessed a change in the way Mennonites, or some Mennonites, regard and interpret our confessional statements. For example, the Ministerial Information Center reserves "the right to exclude persons from the [the Ministerial Information Center] Register if the candidate shows theological incompatibility with the *Confession of Faith in a Mennonite Perspective*. This could suggest

---

[67] The term Luke uses is φρόνησις ([*phronēsis*]; cf. Eph. 1:8), which in Aristotle means practical wisdom or practical reasoning (*Metaphysics* 1142a25–29). On biblical interpretation as practical reasoning, see Stephen E. Fowl, "Authorial Intention in the Interpretation of Scripture," in *Between Two Horizons: Spanning New Testament Studies and Systematic Theology*, ed. Joel B. Green and Max Turner (Grand Rapids: W. B. Eerdmans, 2000), 71–87, esp. 76.

[68] Compare, for example, *The Christian Fundamentals* of 1921, the *Mennonite Confession of Faith* of 1963, and the *Confession of Faith in a Mennonite Perspective* of 1995, each of which claims continuity with Dordrecht.

that the candidate is not suitable for ministry."[69] Indeed it could suggest as much, and the Ministerial Information Center has embraced the difficult task of discerning when theological disagreement amounts to theological incompatibility and unsuitability. Still, the juridical authority it here assigns to the *Confession of Faith in a Mennonite Perspective* (*CFMP*) remains striking—especially so, since a candidate who cannot articulate some degree of theological incompatibility with the *CFMP* may also be unsuitable for ministry. While it stands as a worthy successor to the Dordrecht and Ris confessions, and I regard it as a gift to the church, the *CFMP* contains moments of doctrinal incoherence; it lacks an article on the first person of the Trinity, for example.

Regardless, church-wide concerns about sexuality, and specifically about homosexuality, have provoked a new but limited sense of confessional vigilance.[70] Sometimes, these concerns either reflect or justify themselves as a larger concern about the authority of Scripture. In either case, they have elevated homosexuality, especially the recognition of gay/lesbian covenanted relationships, to *status confessionis*: a matter on which the church's identity as authentically the church of Jesus Christ is at stake and, hence, as an issue properly acknowledged as and required to be church dividing.[71]

Prior to 1995, Mennonite statements on sexuality at Saskatoon '86 and Purdue '87 served to articulate the church's stance on sexuality. The publication of the *CFMP* added another confessional document to which appeal could be made. The *CFMP* does not expressly mention homosexuality, but it affirms that marriage is between one man and one woman, and that "right sexual union" is reserved to marriage so defined (Article 19). In this it follows the earlier statements, whose concluding paragraphs urge a "loving dialogue." Some have understood the sense of this urging to mean that, while a majority of delegates at Saskatoon and

---

[69] Quoting The Ministerial Information Center, Mennonite Board of Congregational Ministries, AS:kh/0496.

[70] Neither the Ministerial Information Center nor any other church body or agency has demonstrated an interest in policing conformity to the *CFMP*. Mennonite pastors and congregations routinely speak or act in opposition to Article 12, which restricts the invitation to the Lord's Supper to those who are baptized.

[71] Within more or less recent memory, the Confessing Church in Germany (Barmen) saw National Socialism as *status confessionis*, as the Dutch Reformed churches did nuclear armaments, and several churches did apartheid.

Purdue approved the statements as expressing the church's theologically and biblically proper stance on the issue, people on both sides should continue to engage in loving, presumably biblical-theological, dialogue about it. In November of 1995, the Mennonite Church Council on Faith, Life, and Strategy issued a statement, "Regarding the Purdue '87 Statement," ruling this interpretation illicit.[72] The CFLS statement has, in the first place, an intended effect: it forecloses dialogue about the meaning of Purdue '87 and about the principal issue—homosexuality—that prompted it.[73] It does not specifically rule out dialogue, but places it in the context of pastoral care "in terms of biblical teaching on the denomination's position" (#3). In other words, "loving dialogue" shall take the form of pastoral care whose goal is the persuasion that the church's position is biblical. This conforms to the statement's ruling that the Mennonite Church's "clearly stated" position (Purdue '87) is biblical (#2). The statement has, then, a second, perhaps unintended, effect: the

---

[72] "Statement by the Mennonite Church Council on Faith, Life, and Strategy Regarding the Purdue '87 Statement, November 19, 1995," *Gospel Herald*, December 12, 1995. The text of this statement reads:

1. The document on human sexuality of Purdue '87 is the position of the Mennonite Church.
2. CFLS affirms this position statement of the Mennonite Church and its General Board.
3. The Mennonite Church's position in this statement is both clearly stated and biblical.
4. The words "loving dialogue" found in this document should not be construed to mean that the homosexual issue is unresolved or that the position of the church is in question.
5. Rather, "loving dialogue" relates to the area of pastoral care in terms of biblical teaching on the denomination's position, care of families and individuals who are touched by this issue, admonitions to those with a homosexual orientation, sponsorship of ministries that are directed toward calling persons out of homosexual practices and restoration in the body of believers, and dialogue that reflects the love of Jesus.

We encourage the church and its leaders to teach in an affirmative way the position of the denomination and not let it go by default. It is our sincere desire to speak with biblical understanding and Christlike compassion. We commend this understanding to the Mennonite Church.

[73] Both Saskatoon '86 and Purdue '87 speak only of homosexual (Purdue: "genital") acts, which they proscribe *only* by way of proscribing all sexual (Purdue: "genital") acts outside the "marriage covenant." Differences between the two statements merit further consideration.

church no longer has any need to consult and study Scripture on this issue, except and unless this consultation will be guided by the assumption that what the Mennonite Church stated, in 1987, is and will remain biblical; and except and unless such consultation and study aim—in the context of "pastoral care"—to lead someone to embrace this assumption as both true and irreversible. In this way, the CFLS statement forecloses further biblical interpretation.[74]

In my view, this marks a significant change in the direction of the Catholic magisterial polity I described above. The CFLS statement severely restricts dialogue, since it does not permit "the position of the church" to be brought into question. Moreover, the statement permits no further inquiry into the question whether the current position of the church is biblical. Rather, the church's confessional document and hence the church's position, as stated by the CFLS, determines, on this matter, what is biblical. The CFLS statement thereby collapses the distinction between Scripture and its juridical interpretation. This marks a significant departure from Mennonite tradition and belief as confessed in the *CFMP,* as I hope now to show.

It is common in some traditions to regard the church's creeds and confessions as a kind of hermeneutical guide or lens for the interpretation of Scripture. The *CFMP,* in its introduction, says something similar in asking "How do Mennonite confessions of faith serve the church? First, they provide guidelines for the interpretation of Scripture" (8). This would seem to concur with the CFLS statement, which sets out authoritative guidelines for the interpretation of confessional guidelines. However, the *CFMP* goes on to say, in its next sentence, "At the same time, the confession itself is subject to the authority of Scripture."

This could be understood in at least two different ways. First, it could be taken to mean that, since the confession is *in fact* grounded in Scripture, it shares in Scripture's authority, if only in a derivative way. This, again, would concur with the view expressed in the CFLS statement. But, second, the *CFMP* could be taken to mean that the confession itself remains subject to correction and revision on the basis of Scripture's singular authority. This is clearly the only legitimate way to read the *CFMP,* given what it says in context, and what it says about its own context.

---

[74] I am characterizing the text of the CFLS statement, not the motives or intentions of its authors and sponsors.

The *CFMP* locates itself within a confessional tradition, or within two such related traditions that it unites. Constituent in this tradition are the historic or ecumenical creeds, which "are basic to" the *CFMP* as well (7). But the tradition also includes a long series of Anabaptist and Mennonite confessions of faith, beginning with Schleitheim's articles, which "the Mennonite Church still recognizes" (7). Also included are the Ris Confession, that of Dordrecht, and later ones, up to and including the Mennonite Confesssion of Faith (1963). Obviously, the *CFMP* departs, at various points, from each of these previous confessions, with which it associates itself as one among a series of "Statements of what Mennonites have believed" (7). It does not repudiate these earlier articles, confessions, and statements, but "takes its place in this rich confessional history" (7). It is a history that includes change of the sort that requires new confessions from time to time, presumably—as the *CFMP* puts it—"subject to the authority of the Bible" (8). For example, the same Bible, with the same authority, in 1963 warranted an article requiring the "veiled head" for women (Article 14), while in 1995 it did not. This conclusion was reached after further inquiry into Scripture—of course, not only after inquiry into Scripture, but also that—and following lengthy, perchance sometimes loving dialogue. The 1963 confession, including Article 14 and its authoritative invocation of "the order of creation," remains part of our confessional tradition, and the *CFMP* at least implicitly recognizes the qualification of its own authority by locating itself within and as a part of this living tradition. Its statements, too, are subject to change: to correction and to revision.[75]

I return, then, to the *CFMP*'s suggestion that it and other confessions provide "guidelines for the interpretation of Scripture." This seems to me to be true. And it is also true that, say, Dordrecht and Ris provide somewhat different guidelines, different from each other and, in turn, from those provided by the *CFMP*. These differences are surely due, in some small part at least, precisely to the interpretation of Scripture that the confessions implicitly or explicitly commend. That is, they commend themselves as interpretations of Scripture, never as replacements of Scripture; and, whether implicitly or explicitly, they commend the interpretation of Scripture even in the course of providing

---

[75] The *CFMP* does not fully acknowledge confessional change and revision: it says only that "confessions give an updated interpretation of belief and practice in the midst of changing times" (8). This obscures the evident fact that not just times but belief and practice change.

guidelines for it. Further, in any such interpretation, the guidelines (i. e., the confessions) by which it is undertaken may prove themselves to be inadequate and in need of revision. I propose that, not only is this exemplified in Mennonite tradition, but that it is constitutive within it: Every confessional statement, every confession of faith, demands to be tested by Scripture, whose interpretation it constitutes and also at the same time commends. Otherwise, it is not a Mennonite confessional statement, and it is "not ...in any wise binding upon the conscience" of believers (Ris, Article 24).

The *CFMP* acknowledges as much, in its Article 4, on Scripture: "We [the church and those who write its confessions] participate in the church's task of interpreting the Bible and of discerning what God is saying in our time by examining all things in the light of Scripture" (22). The very first biblical text cited in support of this statement (of which the statement is thus an interpretation, and for whose interpretation it provides guidelines) is Acts 15:13–20. This text reports the agonizing, but clearly loving, dialogue among the church's first leaders about the inclusion of Gentile converts—converts to Jesus, but not to Judaism. In v. 15, James concludes that Peter's argument "agrees with the words of the prophets." This astonishing agreement depended on a reading of the prophets that departed significantly from the guidelines James and the council he spoke for had inherited. James did discern what God was saying in his time by examining the matter in the light of Scripture; and he found, as did the whole council, that Scripture was saying something utterly unprecedented in the church's young life, something the prophets' words had never "said" before.

I am not here advocating one way or another on the nettlesome issues of sexuality. Rather, I am advocating with the *CFMP* for *sola scriptura*—for the traditional Mennonite idea that anything and everything the church says and does as the church of Jesus Christ, its foundation and head, both constitutes an interpretation of Scripture and demands its interpretation. Such interpretation proceeds with all of the resources that the quadrilateral includes, and more. Nothing the church says or does may be taken as foreclosing the continuing interpretation of Scripture, or else it is not the church that says or does it.

To this point, at the conclusion of this long essay, I have omitted mention of something that the quadrilateral itself omits, which *sola scriptura* doctrines also tend to omit, but which figures mightily in our history and in Acts 15, namely, the Holy Spirit. Peter proclaimed that God had testified to Gentile believers by giving them the Holy Spirit

(Acts 15:8). At the end, James credited the council's remarkable decision to a consensus that the apostles shared with the Holy Spirit. And the apostles reached their decision after hearing testimonies—testimonies to the unprecedented work God was doing among Spirit-gifted Gentiles. Here we have a complete circle. Trustworthy witnesses gave testimony to the work of the Spirit. The witnesses were trustworthy, because their words and their lives agreed with Spirit-inspired Scripture and the gospel. Because the apostles were steeped in Scripture and the gospel, they recognized the work of the Spirit. The testimony of witnesses to that work led the apostles to interpret Scripture as they had never done before.[76] The work of the Holy Spirit—God's work—does not restrict itself to any prevailing consensus, ecclesiastical decision, or scholarly opinion on Scripture's meaning. If this were not so, there never would have been a Christian on earth, much less a Mennonite. To recognize the winds of the Spirit, familiar or fresh, requires the wisdom of saints—of people whose hearts and minds, whose words and lives, are formed by Scripture, and in this way by that same Spirit, who testifies to the church's one foundation. But how will *we* recognize saints?

In Eph. 5:26-27, Christ's presentation of the church without spot or wrinkle is the consequence of Christ cleansing the church "with the washing of water by the word" (ῥήματι [*rhēmati*]). Nothing the church says or does or achieves will substitute for this ablution by verbal immersion. Eph. 6:17 identifies this word (ῥῆμα [*rhēma*]) as the word of God, which it then describes as the sword of the Spirit—the only offensive weapon in the church's arsenal. A Mennonite ecclesiology will orient itself to the sword, whose point is the gospel of peace (6:15).[77]

---

[76] I highly recommend Stephen Fowl's discussion of "How the Spirit Reads/How to Read the Spirit," in *Engaging Scripture: A Model for Theological Interpretation* (Malden, Mass.: Blackwell Publishers, 1998), esp. 101-19, which treat Acts 10-15.

[77] I am grateful to Peter Dula for his vigorous and instructive critique of this essay's first draft.

6

Mennonites and the Church Universal: A Critical Engagement with Miroslav Volf

A. James Reimer

THEOLOGICAL FOUNDATIONS

The Christian doctrine of God is the starting point for all theological and ethical reflection. It should also be the foundation for any thinking about the church.

The first article of the Apostles' Creed asserts the absolute transcendence of God, the unbegotten and uncreated origin of all things visible and invisible (God the Creator).[1] It is the notion of the divine as distinct from creation, as its unbegotten origin, that is here the essential theological claim.

The second article confesses belief in God's only Son. Implicit in it is the claim that the eternal Word (*logos*), identified in the first verses of Genesis as the principle of differentiating order in creation, and in the Wisdom literature as "lady wisdom" (*sophia*), incarnates itself historically in Jesus the Christ. While the first article stresses the transcendence (beyondness) of the divine reality, the second highlights the historicity of that divine reality, its incarnational specificity in time

---

[1] See the Apostles' Creed, in John H. Leith, ed., *Creeds of the Churches*, 3rd ed. (Atlanta: John Knox Press, 1982), 24. The gender-specific component of the affirmation "I believe in God the Father almighty" is relative to the ancient identification of transcendence with the male. What is not relative is the notion behind this gender-specific language—namely, the firm belief that the first person of the Trinity refers to the God who is separate from the created order, in contrast to the deities of the pagan nature religions. Because language is dynamic, and because sexuality itself evolves, there is no guarantee that fatherhood continues to represent transcendence as it did for the ancients. It is conceivable, for instance, that in the future the father image might have an immanentist connotation and "mother" might represent transcendence. Consequently, it is theologically unsound to absolutize the father image in the first article. Not only is it unwise to do so, it is idolatrous, contravening the Hebraic conviction that God is beyond all form.

and space. In the second article the danger of idolatry is present, the risk of equating "God" with the man Jesus of Nazareth. The ancient trinitarian and christological debates revolved around how best to avoid such idolatrous claims. To assert the deity of Christ is to claim that in the being and work of Jesus the Christ—in his conception, birth, life, teachings, ministry, death, resurrection, ascension—the God of the Jews (Yahweh) was manifest, and was experienced by those who responded in faith and life.[2]

The third article affirms belief in the Holy Spirit, and in a series of sub-doctrines (the holy catholic church, the communion of the saints, the forgiveness of sins, the resurrection of the body, and the life everlasting). It is most appropriately understood as confessing the dynamic, life-giving, quickening immanence of the divine reality present within all of creation, but in a particular leavening (or sacramental) way in the community of believers (the church), the "first fruits" of the resurrection of the world.

These three Christian affirmations about the divine reality are confessions about the one true God who has a plurality within unity, in such a way that the one God can be said to be all three simultaneously: transcendent, historical, and immanent.

Twentieth-century discussions of the Trinity by Karl Barth, Jürgen Moltmann, Wolfhart Pannenberg, Miroslav Volf and others, have made much of the distinction and the close connection between the immanent Trinity (the relations among the three persons eternally within God) and the economic Trinity (the relation of God in God's threefoldness to what is external to God, the world). One can give important theological reasons for maintaining a belief in the immanent Trinity as distinct from and as the ground for the economic Trinity, and one can draw on biblical texts to make inferences about immanent trinitarian relations. Yet it appears to me that most of the claims the above theologians make about the immanent Trinity are highly speculative; it is astonishing how much they seem to know about the relations of the three persons within God. My own statements about the Trinity (above), and their application to a doctrine of the church (below), fall into the category of the economic Trinity: our understanding of God's ways with the world. In particular I am concerned with a Christian doctrine of the church from a pneumatological perspective.

---

[2] While Jesus of Nazareth was of male gender, the eternal Christ that was manifest in him is not gender exclusive.

My purpose in what follows is to give some tentative suggestions about what an ecumenically open ecclesiology might look like for Mennonites. This ecclesiology would respect both the plurality and the unity of the global Christian community, both the distinctives that each tradition brings to the ecumenical table, and what all have in common. In what follows I will critically engage the thought of Miroslav Volf on the subject of a Free Church ecclesiology, particularly as he is in conversation with Joseph (Cardinal) Ratzinger and Metropolitan John D. Zizioulas. I will conclude with a proposal of my own, drawing on the views of Anabaptist theologian Balthasar Hubmaier, and on the Apostle Paul's "one body, many gifts" model, which offers creative possibilities for an ecumenical Mennonite ecclesiology.

MIROSLAV VOLF: CONGREGATIONAL CATHOLICITY

In his tour de force, *After Our Likeness: The Church as the Image of the Trinity*, Miroslav Volf develops his own Free Church version of the church as a viable alternative to Roman Catholic and Eastern Orthodox ecclesiologies.[3] He takes Joseph (Cardinal) Ratzinger, Prefect of the Vatican Congregation for the Doctrine of the Faith, as representative of Catholic ecclesiology, and Metropolitan John D. Zizioulas as spokesperson for Orthodox ecclesiology. His theological sparring partner for Free Church theology is John Smyth (1554–1612), early English separatist and (for Volf) the originator of the Free Church. His choice of Smyth as Free Church representative—with no reference to continental Anabaptism and its quite different ecclesiology—is dubious,[4] but serves Volf well as he seeks to build a theology of the church that avoids the weaknesses he sees in Smyth. The great contribution of Volf's work is his serious treatment of Ratzinger and Zizioulas, and his apology for a congregational theology and polity that takes especially Ratzinger's criticisms into account.

---

[3] Volf maintains that he intends to offer a Free Church model of the church not as the best or the only possible understanding, but as at least one legitimate option. This assertion is not altogether convincing because in the end he does appear to propose his congregational alternative as the theologically most justified approach (Miroslav Volf, *After Our Likeness: The Church As the Image of the Trinity* [Grand Rapids: William B. Eerdmans Publishing Co., 1998], 253).

[4] See footnote 33 below.

Ratzinger's Catholic Ecclesiology

For Ratzinger, Christ (the new Adam) is a corporate reality, not an individual one.[5] The Church as the Body of Christ is a single whole, a subject with Christ.[6] The corporate reality of the church always takes precedence over the individual subject. The consequence, according to Volf, is that in Ratzinger's thought the subjectivity and the rights of the individual remain obscure if not nonexistent.[7] The fundamental structure of the ecclesial community is the "being from" and the "being toward" the universal church.[8] As far as church polity is concerned, the local congregation receives its being from the universal church. The universal church is always prior to the local church. The local assembly has the Lord totally through the celebration of the Eucharist, but always in a receptive mode. Every local church derives its catholicity from the universal church, which antecedes and sustains it.

How is this divine reality mediated from the universal church to the local church? Through the office of the bishop. In the person of the properly consecrated bishop, the faith of Christ is transmitted to the local congregation and to the individuals in that congregation.[9] The "primacy of reception" operates on every level of Ratzinger's ecclesiology: in the local church, the liturgy, the individual Christian, the bishop.[10] Volf questions Ratzinger's assumption that anything not based on such a sacramentalism (as, for example, Free Church ecclesiology) must be seen

---

[5] Although Volf does not make this point, in this regard Ratzinger falls in the ancient realist camp (as opposed to the nominalist): invisible universals are real, and the reality of the particulars/individuals lies in their participation in the universal. In contrast, the Free Church tradition, including Volf, falls in the voluntaristic/nominalist tradition, where the individual/particular acting subject is more real than the universal. In this latter tradition, God, and the three divine persons within God, tend to be viewed as individual acting agents. I have in recent years sought to retrieve some modified forms of realism in my theology. In my view, Volf's theology is too nominalistic (as is most contemporary theology).

[6] Volf, *After Our Likeness*, 33.

[7] Ibid., 38, 72.

[8] Ibid., 39.

[9] Ibid., 56–59.

[10] Ibid., 64.

as "self-constructed."[11] What protects the Free Church from this kind of reductionism is its understanding of the Holy Spirit at work in the church. Is not Ratzinger's own hierarchical sacramentalism just as vulnerable to the charge of self-construction? Volf asks.

Ratzinger's ecclesiological "wholism" is based on a view of divine trinitarian personhood as "pure relationality." Standing firmly in the Western tradition, Ratzinger stresses the unity of the Trinity (the dominance of the one divine substance) over the plurality. The differentiation among the persons is nothing more than relational. Since Christ is the prototype of all human personhood, and since the goal of Christ is to integrate all individual persons into the divine trinitarian life of God, in the end the subjectivity and rights of the individual and the local congregation are overwhelmed by a concern with totality, the whole.

In my own reading of Ratzinger's book, I was astonished at the vehemence with which he refers to Free Church ecclesiology. This vehemence is fuelled by an obvious fear that contemporary, post-Vatican II Catholicism is moving in the Free Church direction. There is a crisis in Catholic ecclesiology, he observes. Many, even bishops, are attracted to a North American type of Free Church ecclesiology in which church tends to be a human project, the "Gospel becomes the *Jesus project*, the social-liberation project or other merely historical, immanent projects."[12] Although Free Church ecclesiology does not necessarily understand the church primarily in socio-anthro-political terms (Volf has made this clear, as we will see below), there is something within the voluntarist tradition that can easily lead in that direction, and I found myself agreeing with at least some of his criticisms of Free Church ecclesiology. I was not persuaded by his alternative, however. In particular, I differ with the hierarchical conclusions he draws for church polity.

Ratzinger contrasts this understanding of the church as a human project with the ecclesiology of the Catholic Church, which views itself as "a *more than human* reality, in which reformers, sociologists, organizers have no authority whatsoever."[13] According to Ratzinger, it has a human exterior which constantly needs reform, but behind this

---

[11] Ibid., 65.

[12] Joseph Ratzinger with Vittorio Messori, *The Ratzinger Report: An Exclusive Interview on the State of the Church* (San Francisco: Ignatius Press, 1985), 46.

[13] Ibid.

exterior is the divine reality. It is in its essence the body of Christ. This is its New Testament character. This image is more distinctive for the church than the image of people of God, which gives it its continuity with the Old Testament. "One is Church and one is a member thereof, not through a sociological adherence, but precisely through incorporation in this Body of the Lord through baptism and the Eucharist."[14]

For Ratzinger, this translates into a hierarchical polity: "But the Church of Christ is not a party, not an association, not a club. Her deep and permanent structure is not *democratic* but *sacramental*, consequently *hierarchical*. For the hierarchy based on the apostolic succession is the indispensable condition to arrive at the strength, the reality of the sacrament. Here authority is not based on the majority of votes; it is based on the authority of Christ himself, which he willed to pass on to men who were to be his representatives until his definitive return. Only if this perspective is acquired anew will it be possible to rediscover the necessity and fruitfulness of obedience to the legitimate ecclesiastical hierarchies."[15]

Volf takes seriously Ratzinger's criticism of the individualism of free church ecclesiology but rejects Ratzinger's hierarchical alternative and develops a version of free church ecclesiology based on an egalitarian, nonhierarchical, communal trinitarianism. He wants to redeem the voluntarism and the egalitarianism of the Free Church from its tendency toward "self-enclosed individualism."[16] Volf develops what he considers a novel view of believers church ecclesiology, seemingly unaware of sixteenth-century continental Anabaptist ecclesiology—which had a non-individualistic, communal understanding of the church, and which, in at least one case, was grounded in an egalitarian, communal doctrine of the Trinity. Early Hutterite Peter Riedemann wrote: "Community means that those who have this fellowship hold all things in common, no one having anything for oneself, but each sharing all things with the others. Just so, the Father has nothing for himself, but everything he has, he has with the Son. Likewise, the Son has nothing for himself, but all he has, he has with the Father and with all who have fellowship with him. All who have fellowship with him, and with each other, have likewise nothing for themselves, but they have all things with

---

[14] Ibid., 47.

[15] Ibid., 49.

[16] Volf, *After Our Likeness*, 3.

their Master and with those who have fellowship with them. Hence, they are one with the Son as the Son is one with the Father."[17]

Zizioulas's Orthodox Ecclesiology

Like Ratzinger (and Riedemann), Zizioulas models the church on the Trinity. Nevertheless, his ecclesiology is grounded in a different understanding of that Trinity. In traditional Eastern fashion, Zizioulas's trinitarianism emphasizes the person more strongly than in Ratzinger's thought. Instead of differentiation within the Trinity consisting of "pure relationality" (as in Ratzinger), divinity is understood in terms of "personhood"; "the person represents the ultimate ontological reality."[18] Personhood means communion. The very concept of personhood rests on the divine communion of Father, Son, and Spirit. This does not, however, translate into egalitarianism on either the divine or the human level. Divine and, consequently, also human communion "is always *constituted and internally structured by an asymmetrical-reciprocal relationship between the one and the many.*"[19]

Sin and the Fall consist of separation, isolation, and individualization. The fallen world is defined not by freedom and personhood but by substance, biology, and the realm of necessity. Salvation is the process of deindividualization and personalization which occurs concretely in the church. Christ, understood as a corporate reality (in this Ratzinger and Zizioulas agree), is person *par excellence*, "a corporate personality who incorporates the many into himself."[20] It is in the church, which in a very real sense is Christ on earth,[21] that this incorporation of the many into the one occurs. This transformation from an isolated individual into a divine person in the church is not merely a moral transformation but an ontological one, mediated through baptism,

---

[17] John J. Friesen, trans. and ed., *Peter Riedemann's Hutterite Confession of Faith*, Classics of the Radical Reformation, vol. 9 (Waterloo, Ont., and Scottdale, Pa.: Herald Press, 1999), 80.

[18] Ibid., 77.

[19] Ibid., 78 (Volf's italics).

[20] Ibid., 84.

[21] One is reminded here of Bonhoeffer's understanding of the church as Christ present. Although Volf refers to Bonhoeffer a number of times, he does not make this comparison explicitly. In Bonhoeffer's thought the identity between Christ and the church is less mystical and ontological, and more concrete, sociological, and historical.

effecting a union of created nature with the uncreated God in Christ. In this transformation the filial relationship between the Son and the Father becomes ours also.[22]

What are the implications for ecclesiology? While for Ratzinger the universal church antecedes the local church and gives it its being, for Zizioulas it is the local church that takes precedence over the universal church. In this regard, there is an interesting congruence between Eastern and Free Church ecclesiology. Even more central than the Mass for the Western church is the Eucharist in Eastern thought.[23] It is, as expected, the critical point of Zizioulas's whole ecclesiology. He understands each celebration of the Eucharist, as does the East generally, as the point where the eschatological gathering is realized in the present. Since the Eucharist is a local event, it is the local congregation that truly represents the universal catholic church. The local church is the whole catholic church every time the Eucharist is celebrated.[24] It stands in collegial communion with other local churches who also are catholic in this sense, but there is no sense (as in Ratzinger) that the universal church has precedence over the local congregation.

The decisive components in the celebration of the Eucharist are the bishop and the people. The bishop is the icon of Christ, the corporate reality standing in for Christ in front of the congregation. He is the *alter Christ* who mediates between God and human beings. The people are

---

[22] Volf, *After Our Likeness*, 88.

[23] In the West the Mass is understood as a repeated reenactment of the sacrifice of Christ. The East understands the Eucharist much more broadly as the celebration of the incarnation—including the whole Christ-event—in which the created order is taken up into the very trinitarian life of God.

[24] Volf describes the Eastern celebration of the Eucharist, paraphrasing and quoting Zizioulas, in the following terms: "Since the eucharistic celebration and the (eschatological) heavenly liturgy represent an identical reality, the structure of the heavenly congregation as described in the Apocalypse—the throne of God and of the Lamb, surrounded by the elders with 'seven spirits' and, before the throne, the 'sea of glass' (Rev. 4:2–6)—serves as the model for the structure of the local church. 'The "place (or throne) of God" in the eucharistic synaxis is occupied in reality by the bishop...who is surrounded by the thrones of the "presbyters" and assisted by deacons, with the people facing him.' The Spirit constitutes the church through the bishop, the presbyters and deacons, and the people in their structured relationships" (Volf, *After Our Likeness*, 108). Volf agrees with those who charge Zizioulas with having an "overrealized eschatology" (Ibid., 101).

important but not on equal terms; they are those who say "Amen." The Eucharist is a strictly bipolar event. As there is a hierarchical, asymmetrical mutuality between the divine persons (with the Father as the monarch), so there is a hierarchical, asymmetrical relationship between the bishop and the laity, and within all human relationships. In Christ, mediated to the local congregation through the bishop in the context of the Eucharist, laity are lifted up into the divine life itself, thereby becoming persons. While there are important differences between the Catholic and Orthodox doctrines of the church, between Ratzinger and Zizioulas, in both cases (according to Volf) the subjectivity and rights of the individual and the local church get lost in a hierarchically structured church polity, where individuals are absorbed into the whole.

Volf's Defense of Free Church Ecclesiology

In his carefully developed doctrine of the church, Volf tries to rescue the Free Church from the two aberrations of which Ratzinger accuses it: individualism ("liberal, personalistic, or existentialist"), and reduction to sociology ("group-dynamic interaction").[25] I restrict myself here to examining three aspects of Volf's theological defense of Free Church ecclesiology: his view of the Trinity, his view of the church and its polity, and his view of catholicity. Then I will turn to my own sympathetic critique of Volf and to my own proposal.

1. Trinity. Volf agrees that Free Churches are inclined toward individualism. In order to avoid this aberration, Volf (like Ratzinger and Zizioulas) models his view of the church on the Trinity itself, but with an awareness of the limits of the analogy. The Trinity ultimately remains a mystery that we as humans cannot imitate but can only worship.[26] Despite the differences between Eastern and Western theology, for both Ratzinger and Zizioulas the inner trinitarian life of God remains asymmetrical, monocentric, and monarchical, with unity preceding and overcoming plurality.[27] In contrast, Volf, following his mentor Jürgen Moltmann at Tübingen, argues that unity and multiplicity are equiprimal in God.[28] Even the unity within God must be understood

---

[25] Ibid., 30.

[26] Ibid., 192.

[27] Ibid., 236.

[28] Ibid., 193.

perichoretically—that is, as the three persons coinhering in each other: "Each divine persons [sic] stands in relation not only to the other persons, but is also as a personal center of action internal to the other persons."[29] There can be no analogy between the one divine identity and the church, only between the egalitarian communion of the three persons within the divinity and a corresponding communion of persons within the church. The trinitarian persons must be understood not as one single subject (God) but as three personal subjects (Father, Son, and Spirit), just as individual members of the church need to be understood as equal subjects.[30]

Where the analogy breaks down is with the concept of perichoresis. Human beings do not coinhere in each other as divine persons do.[31] Despite his earlier cautionary note about the mystery of the divine Trinity, Volf seems to know a surprising amount about the communal nature of inner trinitarian life. Despite his cautions about not trying to draw too direct an analogy between the church and the Trinity, he draws quite closely the analogy between the divine and the human. One wonders whether, in the end, Volf himself does not fall prey to the same error of which he accuses Ratzinger and Zizioulas, namely, that he projects his own understanding of what the Free Church should look like onto the inner nature of God.

2. *The Church and Its Polity.* Volf takes as his starting point for discussing Free Church ecclesiology and polity the *Works* of the English dissenter and "first Baptist" John Smyth,[32] someone from within "the Reformed tradition, from which," he claims, "the Free Churches derive."[33] Volf accepts the basic principle of Smyth's Free Church

---

[29] Ibid., 203.

[30] Ibid., 205–6.

[31] Ibid., 211.

[32] W. T. Whitley, ed., *The Works of John Smyth* (Cambridge: Cambridge Univ. Press, 1915).

[33] Volf, *After Our Likeness,* 270. This is, of course, a questionable assertion, as anyone who had read the literature ought to have known. See Donald Durnbaugh, *The Believers' Church: The History and Character of Radical Protestantism* (Scottdale, Pa.: Herald Press, 1968), 8–22. Durnbaugh discusses the three different views of the origins of the Believers Church—sectarian, Puritan, Anabaptist—and makes a persuasive case for the Anabaptists as the true progenitors of the Free Church movement. Volf at no point acknowledges the sixteenth-century Anabaptists as the possible source for Free Church

ecclesiology, "the fundamental *theological* conviction that *Christ's dominion is realized through the entire congregation.*[34] Christ is present in an unmediated way to the entire local church and to every individual believer in that congregation. His presence does not have to be mediated through the narrow gates of office, as in the theology of Ratzinger and Zizioulas.[35] As the Anabaptists did many years before, Volf takes Matt. 18:20 as his foundational text to define what the church is and where it is manifested: *"Where two or three are gathered in Christ's name, not only is Christ present among them, but a Christian church is there as well."*[36] Two essential conditions for ecclesiality are a common confession of faith, and a common commitment to live in the power of the Spirit. Although the church ought to strive to live "without spot and wrinkle," its ecclesiality does not depend on its holiness but "on the presence of Christ who promised to be there wherever people gather together in his name, believe in him as Savior and acknowledge him as Lord in order to live in the power of the Spirit."[37]

Volf believes he is making a contribution to the Free Church ecclesiology of Smyth in applying Ratzinger's and Zizioulas's notion of the sociality or ecclesiality of salvation to Free Church ecclesiology. No one is saved alone. It is only in the context of the church that salvation

---

ecclesiology, nor does he seem to know of John Smyth's and Thomas Helwys's connection with the Waterlander Mennonites in Amsterdam, prior to the beginning of the first Baptist church by Helwys at Spitalfields in England in 1611–12. These details are important because Volf is critical of the early Free Church ecclesiology and soteriology of Smyth for being too individualistic and not trinitarian enough. In *After Our Likeness,* Volf refers to the Anabaptists only once, in a footnote, and names them with the English Separatists (ibid., 132, n. 19). The name of John Howard Yoder also appears only once, with that of James W. McClendon, Jr., and others who seek "to reclaim the communal dimension of the believers' church heritage (ibid., 3). This astonishing oversight on the part of Volf is academically inexcusable, since his own subsequent proposal bears such remarkable similarity to what Anabaptists had said much earlier, and to what his older contemporary John H. Yoder made his life-long preoccupation. Had he taken the Anabaptist tradition more seriously, Volf's claims would seem less novel and would have been modified at a number of important points.

[34] Ibid., 132 (Volf's italics).

[35] Ibid., 152.

[36] Ibid., 136 (Volf's italics).

[37] Ibid., 148.

occurs. But Volf's soteriology differs from that of Ratzinger and Zizioulas; in Volf's view salvation comes not by the church but through the church. This is the crucial distinction. Christ is the only subject of salvific activity, and a direct personal acceptance is required,[38] but the mediation of this salvation is intrinsically communal.[39] What Volf does not seem to realize is that early Anabaptists for the most part saw soteriology ecclesiologically in the same way that he does, as Robert Friedmann argued (not unproblematically) in the early 1970s in his book, *The Theology of Anabaptism*.[40]

3. *Catholicity.* For both Ratzinger and Zizioulas, the church is episcopocentric. The church for Volf is congregation-centered. Furthermore, the congregation modeled after the Trinity is itself polycentric, in contrast to the monocentric church of Ratzinger, and the bipolar church of Zizioulas. Although confession of Christ and commitment to Christ are the defining characteristics of the church, it is the Spirit through her charismata that gives the congregation its inner dynamic. Every person (not different persons through their offices) acts in the power of Christ through the Spirit, who in her sovereignty chooses to allot different gifts and ministries to each member.[41] In both the Roman Catholic Church and the Eastern Orthodox Church there is an "asymmetrical-monocentric distribution of power." The Free Church, on the contrary, presupposes "institutions with symmetrical-decentralized distribution of power and freely affirmed integration."[42]

This ecclesiology is directly linked to Volf's understanding of the Trinity. Volf writes: "The more a church is characterized by symmetrical and decentralized distribution of power and freely affirmed interaction [integration], the more will it correspond to the trinitarian communion."[43] This statement is questionable for two reasons. First, it presumes to know too much about the inner workings of God. Second, despite his earlier caveats in this regard, it draws much too tight an analogy between the divine life and human relationships. In the proposal that follows I prefer

---

[38] Ibid., 164.

[39] Ibid., 162.

[40] Robert Friedmann, *The Theology of Anabaptism* (Scottdale, Pa.: Herald Press, 1973), 78–87.

[41] Volf, *After Our Likeness*, 230–31.

[42] Ibid., 236.

[43] Ibid.

to remain within the realm of the economic Trinity, while not denying the reality of the immanent Trinity and its ultimate antecedence and grounding of any assertions in the realm of "salvation history."

Although Volf wants to distinguish himself from both Ratzinger and Zizioulas, by not excluding the ecclesiology of either the episcopally- or congregationally-understood church, thereby in effect being more catholic than they, in my view he cannot hold his position consistently. He draws the distinction between office holding and its theological justification in the following way: (1) On the level of institutional office holding, he assumes "that Christ can rule in the church both through bishops and through the whole people." He proposes that "the thesis that a participative church structure is the only correct one for all times and places is just as false as the thesis that the hierarchical church structure is God's unalterable decree."[44] (2) On the level of theological justification, Volf makes what appears to be a contrary claim: "This applies even if the strictly *theological* arguments with which the hierarchical understanding of church organization is justified are in *every* context false (which, with regard to a participative understanding of church organization, is not the case)."[45] It appears that Volf wants it both ways: to be fully tolerant of all church polities and at the same time to be theologically convinced of the correctness of the congregational participative model. One reason this dilemma becomes a problem for Volf is that he wants to theologically justify church polity ontologically, i.e., to ground polity in the very inner being of God. In the end, this asks the very human, external structures and organization of the church to carry far too much theological freight.

That Volf identifies himself with a theologically-justified Free Church congregational model becomes clear toward the end of his study when he writes about the meaning of "catholicity" for a church and for individuals. For him, the episcopal and congregational churches have diametrically opposed views of catholicity: the episcopalians dissolve catholicity into a false totality,[46] while the congregationalists respect multiplicity, diversity, and personal subjectivity. What congregationalism must guard against is falling prey to a false particularism.[47] Full catholicity will be achieved only in the future

---

[44] Ibid., 253.

[45] Ibid. (Volf's italics).

[46] Ibid., 261–62.

[47] Ibid., 270.

eschatological gathering of all the people of God. The catholicity of the local church is always broken and partial, and exists not in an already concretely existing universal church of some kind but rather in anticipation of that future eschatological gathering.[48] In this expectation or anticipation, according to Volf, rests the full catholicity of the local church. There is no need for any reference to a concrete universal church.

For Volf the marks of catholicity do not include the local congregation receiving its being from the universal church (as with Ratzinger), nor does the church need to stand in communion with other local churches through bishops (as with Zizioulas). Instead its catholicity resides simply (1) in an openness to other churches who also anticipate the eschatological gathering, and (2) in fidelity to the apostolic tradition that comes by way of the presence of the Spirit to each and every one.[49] It is at the point of Volf's understanding of the charismata that I now finally proceed to my own specific proposal of how Christians in general and Mennonites in particular might understand their own catholicity.

PROPOSAL: MENNONITES AND THE ECUMENICAL GIFTS OF THE SPIRIT

I accept Volf's point that the Holy Spirit is present to the church as first fruits of the eschatological gathering of the whole people of God, and that in this sense each congregation can only be partially catholic.[50] Although I disagree with his nominalistic and voluntaristic view of the church,[51] and find his teleological-directional eschatology a problem, I also—albeit differently—base my proposal on the notion that every local congregation can be only partially catholic.

Volf does not, however, consistently follow through on this basic insight. He proceeds in effect to argue that full catholicity can reside only in local congregations and in individuals in their communion with others in the local church. This has to do with his understanding of the charismata. He maintains that "the catholicity of charismata thus means that each congregation contains *all* ministries within itself necessary to mediate salvation, and that the totality of its members is the bearer of

---

[48] Ibid., 272.

[49] Ibid., 274–75.

[50] Ibid., 268.

[51] I discussed the realist critique of a nominalist/voluntarist understanding of church in "The Adequacy of Voluntarism in a Voluntaristic Age," in *The Believers Church: A Voluntary Church*, ed. William H. Brackney (Kitchener: Pandora Press, 1998), 135–48.

these ministries. Here catholicity means *the fullness of spiritual gifts allotted to the local church.*"[52] He puts this even more strongly: "The local church is catholic in the full sense," and this without any necessary reference to the universal church.[53]

It is here that my own proposal begins to differ from that of Volf. He is in the end too congregationalist for me. In my view, just as no individual can have all the gifts of the Spirit (Volf would agree), so also no local congregation can have all the gifts of the Spirit. It might be argued that a congregation is a congregation only to the extent that it has sufficient number of gifts, and related ministries, for its existence as church to be theologically justified.

I am more of a realist than Volf appears to be when it comes to an understanding of the universal church. By this I mean that a universal church—consisting concretely and presently of all those believers throughout the world (in whatever tradition) who confess Christ—does really exist and can be referred to as the Body of Christ. All Christian traditions—Catholic, Orthodox, Protestant, Free Church, wherever the apostolic confession of faith in Christ is present—belong to this real, universal church. No one local church, no one denomination, no one tradition (whatever its church polity) can claim to be the exclusive guardian of the Body of Christ. Each is given a set of spiritual gifts that contribute to the body as a whole. I believe Balthasar Hubmaier had this in mind when in his 1528 *Apologia* he referred to the universal church as "mother" and the local congregation as "daughter":

> The church is an outward assembly and community of Christ-believers in one Lord, one faith and one baptism, Eph. 4:4f. It should be noted here that the word *church* is used in the Scriptures for two kinds of church: First, for the universal holy, Christian communion and assembly of all who believe in Christ, wherever on earth they be, in the whole circle of the world. And so we believe in a holy Christian church, which is a community of the saints. Christ also speaks of the church in this sense, Matt. 16:18. This church is the body of Christ. Christ is the head and we are the members of the body of Christ, 1 Cor. 12; Eph. 2; 4; Col. 1; 3. Second, the church is understood in the Scriptures as a particular community of some believers in Christ, such as the church of the Galatians, Gal. 1, the church of the Corinthians, 1 Cor. 1. This refers to each believing parish populace of a town,

---

[52] Volf, *After Our Likeness*, 273.

[53] Ibid., 274.

marketplace, or village, as one also finds in Ephesians 1. It is this specific congregation that is commonly called the daughter and the general church the mother. Now the daughter has equal authority with the mother, which is the general church, to bind and to loose sin according to Christ's command, as the Scripture testifies concerning the Corinthian church, 1 Cor. 5; 2 Cor. 2. This authority the particular church now commends and gives over to its chosen, established, and ordained minister and priest, so that all things may be done in an orderly manner. *Both of these churches are outward communities and not imaginary, conceivable, or logical essences*, as I explained in my booklets on the catechism, on brotherly discipline, and on the ban.[54]

My proposal builds on Hubmaier's organic understanding of the universal church as mother and the local church as daughter, both concretely existing communities, but one a part of the whole. I go beyond Hubmaier in at least one sense: I apply Paul's explication of the gifts of the Spirit in 1 Corinthians 12 to the way the relationship of a local church/denomination to the universal church might be understood. A second point at which I might go beyond Hubmaier, although I will not do so in this context, is where he gives full powers of church discipline to a local congregation. There is a third point at which I part company with Hubmaier: I do not believe his view of the universal church as purely a concrete, visible community of presently-existing believers throughout the world is an adequate one. Here my realism contrasts with Hubmaier's nominalism: There is a sense in which the universal church is an invisible reality behind the concretely existing universal church. It is that invisible community of those who have come before us and will come after us who confess the Christ.

Three New Testament texts list gifts of the Spirit: Rom. 12:4–8 (prophecy, service, teaching, exhortation, contribution, giving aid, acts of mercy), Eph. 4:11–16 (apostles, prophets, evangelists, pastors, teachers), 1 Cor. 12:1–26 (wisdom, knowledge, faith, healing, miracles, prophecy, discernment, tongues, interpretation). The fact that these lists are all different, though they have similarities, suggests that none of the congregations Paul is writing to has a comprehensive set of gifts that

---

[54] "Apologia," in *Balthasar Hubmaier: Theologian of Anabaptism*, trans. and ed. H. Wayne Pipkin and John H. Yoder (Scottdale, Pa., and Kitchener, Ont.: Herald Press, 1989), 546–47 (my italics).

makes it totally self-sufficient.[55] From the start, congregations in the different centers of the Greco-Roman world (Jerusalem, Alexandria, Antioch, Constantinople, Rome, Ephesus, Corinth, etc.) had their own individual character, and developed different theological orientations out of which emerged different historical traditions. This is already evident in these letters and in the gifts that Paul identifies in each. What the three lists have in common is the call for humility, love, and unity in the light of this diversity.

The most comprehensive set of gifts is the one found in Paul's letter to the Corinthians. He describes the spiritual charisms given to individual Christians in Corinth not as their own possession but as belonging to the community. He envisions the church as an organic body with each of the organs (those that appear weaker as well as those that seem stronger) being indispensable parts of the whole. In fact, "God has so adjusted the body, giving the greater honor to the inferior part, that there may be no discord in the body, but that the members may have the same care for one another" (12:24–25). The whole point is that while there is a diversity of gifts, there is one Lord, one Spirit, one God (12:4–6).

Customarily we think of these various charisms given to a particular congregation as the spiritual basis for the different ministries on the local level. This is also how Volf interprets the gifts of the Spirit. I believe, however, that we can, without doing an injustice to these New Testament texts, apply these gifts to the various larger theological traditions within the universal church (as Hubmaier thinks of it). I am not seeking to draw a strict parallel between each of the separate gifts itemized by Paul and a specific Christian tradition. Rather, I suggest that each of the major Christian groups contributes a valuable emphasis to the Christian body as whole, an emphasis that has a biblical basis and is pneumatically given: *Eastern Orthodoxy,* the church as the mystical body of Christ Pantocrator, the Lord of the Universe (Eph. 1:15–23); *Roman Catholicism,* the historic, institutional church as the official guardian of the tradition through the apostolic succession and the sacraments (Matt. 16:13–20); *Anglicanism,* worship and liturgy (the Psalms, Isaiah 6); *Lutheranism,* justification by grace through faith (Gal. 3:6–14); *Calvinism,* the sovereignty of God, covenant, election, and the cultural mandate (2 Pet. 1:10; Rom. 9:6–18; Gen. 1:27–28, 2:15–17); *Methodism,* holiness and sanctification (1 Pet. 1:13–21); *Anabaptists/Baptists,* church

---

[55] For this observation I am indebted to John Toews, scholar of the book of Romans and President of Conrad Grebel College.

as voluntary, gathered community (Matt. 18:15–20); *Quakers,* quiet meditation and spontaneous worship based on light within (1 Cor. 14:26–33); *Pentecostalism,* gifts of the Spirit, especially glossolalia (Acts 2:1–4); *Mennonites,* discipleship and the historic peace witness (Matt. 5; Rom. 12:9–21).

This is not meant to be an exhaustive list but it does illustrate my point. I do not mean to suggest that these emphases are exclusive to one tradition, nor that they exhaust the gifts of that tradition, but rather that they are highlighted by that tradition. Furthermore, the whole body of Christ, the universal Christian community (in Hubmaier's understanding of the term) needs all of these gifts for its wellbeing. None can do without the other. This way of looking at the relationship of the local church to the universal church allows for diversity without relativism, and unity without dogmatism. The question might be asked: Is any one of these emphases (gifts) incompatible with any other? As I have identified them above, I do not think so, but it would take more space than I have here to explore that question in sufficient theological depth. The *sine qua non* would be confession of one God, one Lord, one Spirit.

CONCLUSION: IMPLICATIONS FOR MENNONITES

Certain implications for confession, church polity, and ethics follow from the above proposal. In my view, there is a reverse hierarchy, a gradation of levels, from the more general (the universal church level) to the more particular (congregational level). The lowest level is the foundational level at which universal consensus is critical. At the highest level, because it is farthest from the theological core of the confession, agreement is not as critical. Alternatively, one could visualize a central core, with ever larger concentric circles around it. Core theological/confessional issues that all Christians have in common include affirmation of the Christian doctrine of God as Creator, Christ, Spirit. This properly belongs on the universal level. Structural questions of polity, and certain historical theological distinctives would be located on the denominational level.

The recent integration of the Mennonite Church and the General Conference Mennonite Church on the denominational level can (in my view) be justified theologically, but the division of the denomination into two nations (Canada and United States) cannot be. There may be good pragmatic and sociological reasons for that division, but it raises the question of what theological significance nationality has for Christians.

Particular matters about which sincere Christians (who confess the faith in the one God, the one Christ, and the one Spirit) find themselves in honest disagreement even within a denomination would be dealt with on a local, congregational level (e.g., homosexuality). Disagreements between denominations (second level) or between congregations (third level) do not justify excommunication or schism, where schism is defined as separation from the universal body of Christ (as understood above). This does not mean that the second and third levels do not have theological relevance, just that the farther you move away from the core, the less foundational are the matters dealt with at that level.

What are the specific implications of this proposal for Mennonites and their historic peace witness? One communion's gift is an essential aspect of the whole, but it is not the whole. One definition of heresy, using this model, would be the reduction of all gifts to one's own gift, and the absolutization of that gift as though it were the total truth. No one tradition embodies the fullness of all the gifts; to attempt to do so would dilute each gift and would be a sure way to lose the singular power of that gift. The Mennonite emphasis on discipleship and peace (variously named nonresistance, pacifism, nonviolence) is one gift among many, but it is an essential one for the whole church. To understand its peace emphasis as a "gifted" ministry to the whole body of Christ is more than a vocation (as, for example, "vocational pacifism"). It is a truth that applies to the whole body. The Spirit working through this particular tradition is transforming the entire body and bringing the resurrection of the entire world. However, Mennonites must always remember that other gifts that other traditions have are just as important, and maybe more important, in fulfilling God's divine purpose for creation. As I have argued frequently, Mennonite peace witness cannot be the foundation of our theology, although it is intrinsically part of Christian theology. The ultimate foundation is God in God's threefoldness.

7

Polities That Unite and Divide: Magnets and Fences

Lois Barrett

All polities unite and divide. All polities affect who is in (united) and who is out (divided). The question is, How well do various polities help the church deal with both unity and diversity? And how well do various polities put us in right relationship? What effect do these polities have on those inside and those outside the church? What constitutes a good polity for the church?

Looking at the culture around us is not much help. Many people have taken a relativist attitude: there is no absolute truth, only my truth and your truth, and no way to arbitrate between them. On the other hand, some public school districts have adopted zero-tolerance policies regarding violence, and in Kansas recently a high school girl was expelled for a piece of artwork that included some violent language. Moreover, the language of tolerance often gets confused. Is one tolerant when one doesn't use violence to enforce one's own standard of behavior on everyone else, or when one believes that all behaviors and convictions are equally valid, when one is not racist, or when one can "live and let live"? Our society is unsure about what tolerance means.

In terms of church polity, the challenge is to deal with the issues of unity and diversity in ways that maintain right relationships, draw people into relationship with Christ and the church, and disciple people along the way of Jesus, as we know him through Scripture and Spirit.

THE SHAPE OF THE CHURCH

As a political body, the church has structures that define its center and its boundaries, and the church has a culture that influences relationships within those structures.

Polity and the Church

Polity is not a necessary evil, but is central to the shape of the church. Church polity is not an unfortunate necessity, but is vital to the being of the church. In the New Testament as well as the Old, political language is used to describe the church. The saints are citizens of heaven, ambassadors of reconciliation, elders standing around the throne, a holy nation, a royal priesthood, the people of God. Much of this language is borrowed from Exodus, where it describes the nature of the Hebrew people as God's people. Even the word we translate "church," *ekklesia*, is a political word. It can mean any assembly, but in the Greek world it usually meant an assembly of citizens for decision making, a town meeting.

Although Jesus resisted Satan's offer of all the kingdoms of the world, the New Testament pictures the risen Jesus as now above all other rulers and powers. Jesus has a kingdom, but not like the other kingdoms of the world, otherwise "my followers would be fighting to keep me from being handed over to the Jews" (John 18:36). The disciples have trouble understanding power in Jesus' kingdom: "You know that the rulers of the Gentiles lord it over them.... It will not be so among you" (Matt. 20:25). In fact, Jesus' kingdom is greater than the other kingdoms of the world. These other "thrones or dominions or rulers or powers" have been created through him and for him (Col. 2:15–20). For the early Christians, to call Jesus "Lord" was a risky alternative to calling Caesar "lord." In the Synoptic Gospels, the center of Jesus' message is the kingdom of God (kingdom of heaven).

The New Testament contains many other images of the church: a body with many members, a holy temple, a dwelling place for God, a spiritual house, the bride of Christ, branches on the vine. But the pervasiveness of the political images of the church in the New Testament should overcome any hesitancy we might have at thinking about the church in political terms.

Structures As Fences: Defining Boundaries

Boundaries are part of the definition of any group. We might think of boundary church structures as fences. Fences define what is inside the fence (approved behavior for members of the group) and what is outside the fence (behavior that puts you under the discipline of the group).

We see some examples in the New Testament of fences as structures of church polity. In 1 Corinthians, the prohibition on incest acts as a fence; in 2 John, teaching false doctrine is outside the fence; elsewhere, creating factions within the church is a boundary issue.

The congregation of which I used to be pastor came up against a boundary when a woman who had been attending the church and considering membership said one day in a church meeting, "This would be a really good church if you just didn't talk about Jesus quite so much." This was a boundary issue for the church. We weren't willing to quit talking about Jesus.

In a board meeting somewhere in the Mennonite world a few years ago, one board member made a speech in which he attacked another board member. Almost immediately others sitting around him began talking to him and telling him that he had not acted rightly, that he needed to apologize to the person he had wronged, that such behavior was not appropriate for Christians. One of the boundaries defining how we behave in board meetings had suddenly become clear. This was a positive use of a fence.

But we can also misuse the fences of church polity. We can put up fences in the wrong places. We can throw people over the fence. We can refuse to invite people back inside the fence. What purpose do the fences of church polity serve?

First, fences are part of what gives the church identity. We know who we are as a church, in part, because we know the boundaries. We are a church that refuses to participate in the military. We are a church that does not swear oaths of allegiance. We are a church that upholds faithfulness in marriage.

Second, the fences of church polity have a missional purpose. Church discipline is of one piece with evangelism and discipling each other. Church discipline at its best is not a matter of controlling people, but of regaining brothers and sisters when their behavior destroys relationships with God and with others. Thus, church discipline has the same goal as evangelism and the discipling process: bringing people into closer relationship with God through Christ. When the church loses sight of the missional purpose of church discipline, such discipline either becomes harsh and punitive, or weak or nonexistent. In neither case will people be brought into right relationships with God and with the church.

Magnets: Drawing People toward the Center

Although fences are important in defining boundaries, they are not sufficient to define the center of the church. A magnet is an image of the center; it draws to itself all things that are attracted to it. The motion of this image is found in the New Testament in passages like John 12:32: "And I, when I am lifted up from the earth, will draw all people to myself"; and John 6:44: "No one can come to me unless drawn by the

Father who sent me." In the Gospel of John, Jesus is the center, and all who walk in the light will be drawn toward Jesus the light.

So a good church polity will not simply judge whether people are inside or outside the fence. A good church polity will attempt to discern whether people are moving toward the center, whether they are being drawn toward Jesus. The issue here is not how far away from the center they are, but whether they moving in the right direction. Are they letting themselves be drawn to Jesus and his cross?

Again, there is a missional impulse within this magnet image of the church. We want all people to be drawn to Christ. Isaiah 2 has a picture of all the nations streaming to the mountain of the Lord to learn God's ways instead of the ways of war. It is an image of unity. In spite of our diversity, in spite of our different distances from the center, something is holding the church together. We want new believers to be attracted to this magnet. We want those who have been in the church a long time to be drawn closer to Christ.

Statements like the Mennonite Church's "Vision: Healing and Hope" function as magnets.[1] A churchwide commitment to service is a magnet. Before I was a Mennonite, its peace position was a magnet drawing me to the Mennonite church. If all I had known about Mennonites then were the fences, I doubt that I would have become a Mennonite. Mission statements function as magnets. They don't set the boundaries as much as they define the center. When people are clear about the center, a lot of other things fall into place.

So, should our polity be a magnet or a fence? Yes. We need both. If we want to be faithful and effective in our polity, we need to resist choosing between magnets and fences. I have talked to some who grew up only with the fence image of church polity. To compensate, they want to do away with fences and just have magnets. I have talked to others who don't say much that sounds magnetic, but who think that reinforcing the fences will solve the church's problems. If we want to be faithful and

---

[1] "Vision: Healing and Hope" was adopted by the General Assembly (MC) and the Triennial Sessions (GC) meeting at Wichita, Kansas, in 1995. Copies are available from the Mennonite Church USA (421 S. 2nd St., Suite 600, Elkhart IN 46516-3243; phone 219-294-7131; fax 219-293-3977; mcgb@juno.com; or PO Box 347, Newton KS 67114-0347; phone 316-283-5100; fax 316-283-0454; shelleyb@gcmc.org); or from Mennonite Church Canada (600 Shaftesbury Blvd., Winnipeg MB R3P 0M4; phone 204-888-6781; fax 204-831-5675; mail@mennonitechurch.ca).

effective as a missional church, we will have strong magnets, clearly visible both within and outside the church.

We will also have fences that reflect a theology worked out for today in our context in the light of Scripture and Spirit. Context is important for the kind of fence you have and where you put it. You don't need the same kind of fence for horses and chickens. Do you ever put a fence in the middle of a creek? It depends. You may need to move a fence as the situation changes. Wise fence construction calls for continuing theological work on the part of the church community.

THE CULTURE OF THE CHURCH

Fences and magnets are often formal and visible. A less visible expression of church polity is the organizational culture of the church, "the way we do things here." The way we do things, of course, varies from one part of the Mennonite church to another. But three practices of Mennonite culture related to polity are (or should be) pervasive.

Discernment: Consensus or Robert's Rules?

One part of our culture is the way we make decisions. Of course, that happens in many ways. The *Confession of Faith in a Mennonite Perspective* identifies consensus as the preferred way to make decisions:

> Church order is needed to maintain unity on important matters of faith and life so that each may serve and be served, and the body of Christ may be built up in love. Love and unity in the church are a witness to the world of God's love.
>
> In making decisions, whether to choose leaders or resolve issues, members of the church listen and speak in a spirit of prayerful openness, with the Scriptures as the constant guide. Persons shall expect not only affirmation, but also correction. In a process of discernment, it is better to wait patiently for the word from the Lord leading toward consensus, than to make hasty decisions.[2]

In other words, consensus requires seeking God's will, rather than seeking to get our own way. This practice differs from asking God to put a stamp of approval on our decisions.

My experience with consensus decision making over the past 30 years is that the best decisions come when we empty ourselves of our own wants and together seek to hear what God wants. The best decisions

---

[2] *Confession of Faith in a Mennonite Perspective* (Scottdale, Pa., and Waterloo, Ont.: Herald Press, 1995), 62.

also come in a climate of trust and respect. One needs to trust that the other, with whom one disagrees, is also seeking the will of God. If trust and respect are not there, we might as well use Robert's Rules of Order. In fact, if people cannot display trust in and respect for each other, Robert's Rules allows the group to move forward in an orderly way.

The issue is not whether we should decide by consensus or by voting. The question is, How can our polity build the trust and respect that makes consensus possible? How can we build into the life of the denomination and the lives of area conferences and congregations the face-to-face interactions that make possible the development of trust and respect? How can our polity provide opportunities for us to grow in our practice of seeking God's will together?

Agreeing and Disagreeing in Love

I would like to frame and hang these words in every Mennonite office and meeting room, and put them at the top of the letters-to-the-editor column in Mennonite periodicals: "I may disagree with you, but that doesn't mean I don't love you." Or: "I may be your friend, but that doesn't mean I always agree with you or that I always do what you want me to do." Or: "You may disagree with me, but that doesn't mean you are my enemy."

I am trying to excise the word "support" from my vocabulary. One never knows what it means. Does support mean agreeing, or caring? The dictionary definitions of support include propping up something, lending strength to someone, approving, and advocating. During the Gulf War, the U.S. government urged citizens to "support our troops," effectively mixing caring about soldiers as people and approving the conduct of the war. Last summer, I received letters and e-mail messages from people who disagreed with a decision I had made, accusing me of not caring about them. Love and agreement are not the same.

It is inherent in our human condition that we find it difficult to be different from each other while staying connected with each other. If I believed in original sin, I would define it as the desire for everyone around us to be just like us. It is good that babies want to be just like the people with whom they have the closest relationship. That is how children are socialized. But as we grow older, we need to learn how to be in relationship with people from whom we are different. The demand that people around us be just like us is at the heart of racism, sexism, xenophobia, and ethnic cleansing. If we cannot continue to love people around us who are different from us, how will we ever learn to love enemies?

How can we make love the measure of our polity? How can we maintain face-to-face right relationships with people in the church with whom we disagree? How can our structures put us in relationship with people who are in the church but outside our comfort zones? We need to make the practices of the statement "Agreeing and Disagreeing in Love" a part of the way we do things here.[3]

Humility about Being Right

The second sentence I would like to frame is: "Just because they're wrong doesn't mean we're right." Showing up the errors of the other side does not equal proving that our side is in the right. Logically, this seems so obvious, but when we are in conflict it is often not obvious. We tend to assume that there are only two possible positions, one right and one wrong. So if we prove that the other side is somehow in the wrong, then we must be in the right.

It should be a part of the church's culture, one of the ways we do things here, to recognize that truth may lie with more than one party. We may be partly right and partly wrong; they may be right about one part of the issue and wrong about another part of the issue. There may be more than one right way.

Some strands of Mennonite culture in North America have tended to discipline both parties in a destructive conflict, assuming that both sides are at least partly in the wrong—if not in terms of goals, at least in terms of means. This is because "truth" is both true to the facts and true to relationships.

---

[3] "Agreeing and Disagreeing in Love: Commitments for Mennonites in Times of Disagreement" was adopted by the General Assembly (MC) and the Triennial Sessions (GC) meeting at Wichita, Kansas, in 1995; both bodies commend these guidelines to congregations, area conferences, and church-wide agencies. Copies are available from the General Conference Mennonite Church (PO Box 347, Newton KS 67114-0347; phone 316-283-5100; fax 316-283-0454; chm@gcmc.org), from Mennonite Church Canada (600 Shaftesbury Blvd., Winnipeg MB R3P 0M4; phone 204-888-6781; fax 204-831-5675; mail@mennonitechurch.ca); from the Mennonite Church Peace and Justice Committee (PO Box 173, Orrville OH 44667; phone/fax 330-683-6844; mcpjc@sssnet.com) and through Mennonite Resources Network (http://www.mrn.org/ADLove/).

To understand that both of us may be in the wrong and/or in the right is part of the virtue of humility. True humility is not subservience, but finding my right place, putting myself not above the other but beside the other. True humility allows me to laugh at myself. It allows me to listen more carefully to the one with whom I disagree. A right polity will encourage us to call "foul" when people try to prove their rightness by proving the other wrong.

GALATIANS 5:13–6:5

The letter to the Galatians is about fences wrongly placed. Specifically, it is about requiring circumcision for Gentile men who want to come into the church. A main point of Galatians is that new Gentile Christians should be free of that fence. The fence should be removed or moved. Gal. 5:13–6:5 illustrates some of the points above.

In this text the center, the magnet, is stated first: "You shall love your neighbor as yourself." Love is the magnet that draws people together. In fact, if you do not love the neighbor, "you bite and devour one another."

The next section (5:16–21) identifies the fences, the "works of the flesh": everything from fornication, idolatry, and sorcery to quarrels, factions, and envy. All these are put outside the fence; "those who do such things will not inherit the kingdom of God." In this list of 15 works of the flesh, there seems to be no prioritizing of more and less serious sins. All these things are outside the reign of God.

These works of the flesh are contrasted in 5:22–24 with the "fruit of the Spirit": love, joy, peace, patience, kindness, generosity, faithfulness, gentleness, and self-control. The church's polity (reinforced by its organizational culture) must be one that prunes and fertilizes so this fruit will grow.

Discernment about what is of the Spirit and what is of the flesh (the fences) is to be guided by the Spirit (5:25). Humility has high value. "Let us not become conceited." But take care that "if anyone is detected in a transgression, you who have received the Spirit should restore such a one in a spirit of gentleness. Take care that you yourselves are not tempted" (6:1). In the process of disciplining someone else, we must be careful that we also are not in the wrong. Moreover, this discipline has a missional purpose: it is to restore the sinner in a spirit of gentleness.

Polity and Mission

The unity of the church is not an end in itself. The church is called to point beyond itself. The mission of the church is to proclaim and to be a sign of the reign of God. The only unity worth striving for is the unity that makes this mission possible. The ultimate test is not what we here on earth can agree on; the ultimate standard against which all church polity is judged is the reign of God. Can others look at us and see that here is a glimpse of the kingdom of God, albeit incomplete? How does this polity invite people to enter the reign of God? How does this polity help the church in its life together to be a sign of the reign of God?

8

The Church:
Missional Community of the Kingdom

John Driver

INTRODUCTION

Christians have traditionally attempted to define the church by means of lists of characteristics that are considered an essential minimum for the church to be the church. In the Roman Catholic tradition, the church came to be defined as a sacramental community. By implication, saving grace, communicated through the sacraments, could not be experienced outside the church. Following the lead of Martin Luther, Protestants have defined the true church as the locus in which the Word is truly proclaimed and the sacraments are correctly administered. The Calvinist tradition tended to add a third characteristic, the proper exercise of ecclesiastical discipline.

In these definitions, the clergy is essential to the existence of the true church. Among the radical movements of renewal, lists of signs of the true church have tended to be longer, applying to both the life and the mission of the entire Christian community. Menno's list is an example. To (1) the salvific and unadulterated teaching of God's Word, and (2) the scriptural use of the sacraments, he added (3) obedience to God's Word manifested in holiness of life, (4) sincere and unfeigned love for others, (5) faithful confession of Christ's name, will, Word, and ordinance "in the face of all cruelty, tyranny, tumult, fire, sword, and violence of the world," and (6) the cross of Christ borne by all his disciples for the sake of his testimony and Word.[1]

Established Christianity, Catholic as well as Protestant, tended to understand its identity ontologically, in terms of its own essential being or character. Radical or believers church movements of renewal have tended to understand themselves more dynamically, in terms of what they have perceived to be their missional purpose in God's salvific

---

[1] Leonard Verduin, trans., and J. C. Wenger, ed., *The Complete Writings of Menno Simons* (Scottdale, Pa.: Herald Press, 1956), 739–41.

intention. They have been more oriented to the church's God-given mission and less statically fixated on their own unique being. This is the same tension that we find present in the biblical record. While Judaism was often tempted to view its fundamental identity as God's chosen people in terms of special privilege, the prophetic and messianic visions were essentially missional. There was a clear divine call to salvific existence and witness not merely for the people's own sake but for the salvation of "the nations" to be realized under God's righteous reign. Of course, this tension is found not only in the church's history. It is an ongoing temptation, not limited to the established tradition, but present even among those denominations whose spiritual roots can be traced to the radicals of yesteryear.

DEFINITIONS AND EXAMPLES

I am using the term "missional" intentionally. I realize that it may not even be a proper English word. When I began to use *misional* in relation to the church in Latin America, a seminar participant objected that was not really a proper word in the Spanish language. The English-language spell checker on my computer program persists in questioning my usage.

I have been pleased to see the term used with increasing frequency. A 1998 book that emerged out of The Gospel and Our Culture project is entitled *Missional Church: A Vision for the Sending of the Church in North America*.[2] More recently, the Transformation Team of Mennonite Church USA prepared an excellent resource used by many Mennonite congregations during the fall of 1999, "Envisioning a New Mennonite Church: A Study Guide for Mennonite Congregations and Organizations." In it writer Lois Barrett straightforwardly argues that the church is indeed called to be missional. While *mission* may be the reason for the church's existence, and *missions* may refer to activities carried out by the church to fulfill its mission, the church needs to be *missional*. This has to do with the essential nature and vocation of the people charged with carrying out God's salvific intention in the world. "Missional" has to do both with what the church is and with what the church does.

I began to catch a glimpse of what a missional church might be like during our sojourn in Spain in the late '70s and early '80s. During this period, a network of Radical Christian Communities emerged across the

---

[2] Darrell L. Guder, ed., *Missional Church: A Vision for the Sending of the Church in North America* (Grand Rapids: W. B. Eerdmans, 1998).

northern half of Spain. The genesis of these communities, beginning in Burgos, has multiple roots—the witness of young people who were serving under the auspices of Youth with a Mission, charismatic movements within Roman Catholicism, the witness of a Finnish and Uruguayan artist of Pentecostal persuasion, the support and friendship of a few evangelical young people, as well as Mennonite encouragement and initiatives.

In their beginnings, these communities would scarcely have fit the common definitions of church. In fact, Spanish evangelicals took a dim view of them. Early in its history, the community in Burgos had somehow gotten a copy of my book *Comunidad y compromiso,* recently published in Argentina.[3] When a participant in the group appeared at our door in Madrid inviting me to visit and share with them, I asked a leader in the denomination in which I was participating for advice. The gist of his response was that he supposed it would be all right, as long as it did not become common knowledge. Later, a prominent member of the largest Protestant congregation in Barcelona, probably expressing the feelings of evangelicals in general, told me that she couldn't understand how a serious person like me could associate with people like these.

As I have reflected on the emergence of these communities, I am convinced that they were more like the missional communities of the Bible than most of their evangelical or Catholic counterparts. Even as they were emerging with a distinctive identity they began to orient their life around a specific mission to which they felt God was calling them. Without waiting until they were financially or numerically "able," the community in Burgos began a ministry of rehabilitation for victims of the drug culture. During our early visits to the community, we could scarcely distinguish between the healers and those being healed, so humanly precarious did the balance between the two groups appear to us. Before long the community added a prison ministry and became a halfway house for those who were released without a viable opportunity to make a new start, as well as a hospice for those suffering from AIDS.

Another community of faith emerged in one of the outlying barrios of Barcelona. Rather than focusing on their own ecclesial identity, narrowly defined, they asked what gifts for ministry God had placed in

---

[3] John Driver, *Comunidad y compromiso: Estudios sobre la renovación de la iglesia* (Buenos Aires: Ediciones Certeza, 1974); translated under the title *Community and Commitment* (Scottdale: Herald Press, 1976).

their midst. With a minimum of resources, the community built a modest residence for the elderly and dedicated their energies to caring for this sometimes forgotten sector of Spanish urban society. They provided an extended household in which lonely people could spend their last days surrounded by loving and caring brothers and sisters in the family of faith. The worship and the work of this community were integrated in the single reality of their life and faith and witness as a missional community of God's kingdom.

In Galicia, a group emerged out of an evangelical background with a sense of calling to become a community of worship and work. They organized a ceramics cooperative to offer an alternative to the competitiveness so common in the secular workplace. They were a living witness to new possibilities of love, justice, and economic sharing in human relationships that, according to the New Testament, characterize God's kingdom.

In northern Spain, a number of young Catholics formed a community in a village, sharing with one another and showing love and kindness toward their rural neighbors, who were often relegated to the fringes of society. They lived simply and compassionately among their neighbors in their attempt to show what the kingdom of God is like. They were intentional about their sense of mission. In fact, a neighbor with whom my wife, Bonny, was visiting in the village said to her one day, "That Antonio—I have never in my life seen anyone who reminds me so much of Jesus as Antonio does."

And there were other similar groups in this network of Radical Christian Communities. These communities would scarcely have met the minimum definition for being church. None of them began with buildings dedicated exclusively as houses of worship. However, both in symbol and reality, they broke the bread of fellowship together and drank the wine of lives poured out in life-giving sacrifice and service to others. They were, in fact, missional communities of the kingdom.[4]

Some of these communities have survived institutionally, while others have not continued, at least not in their original forms. Admittedly, groups like these have proved difficult to program, but these examples are by no means unique. Similar movements, such as

---

[4] These communities share these characteristics. They (1) are missional; (2) are charismatic in the sense of depending on God's gracious gifts for their common life, nurture and mission; (3) have formal and/or informal sharing of resources; (4) are ecumenical in their relationships of accountability with the wider church.

Missionary Congregations within Roman Catholicism and renewal movements in Protestantism, have arisen throughout Christian history. These have touched my life and taught me something of what it might mean to be a missional church.

Personally, I am convinced that the gospel dictum, so often repeated by the evangelists, is true in a corporate sense as well as in a personal one. "Those who want to save their life will lose it, and those who lose their life for my sake, and for the sake of the gospel, will save it" (Mark 8:35; cf. Matt. 10:39; 16:25; Luke 9:24; John 12:25). This undoubtedly also applies to the church. According to the Gospels, in a strange and mysterious way we find the secret of true life in giving our life for others.

A BIBLICAL VISION OF A MISSIONAL PEOPLE OF GOD

The biblical story begins with creation, a creation that culminates in the formation of a community that bears God's image. Although this communion with God and creation soon fell victim to human ambition, we do get a fleeting glimpse of creation as God intended it, and in the ongoing story we catch a vision of God's strategy for restoration. The human family continues beyond the violence of Cain. In Noah's story, God's mercy prevails in the midst of judgment. When, in the story of Babel, humankind's lust for power reaches a climax and its attempts to dominate end in its own alienation and confusion, God responds with a new creation, a new beginning, the formation of a missional people that again reflects the name and image of God.

This alternative—a people that reflects God's character and expresses, albeit imperfectly, God's salvific intention—is essential to our understanding of the biblical meaning of peoplehood, as well as our understanding of mission. Attempts to recover the biblical vision of peoplehood apart from God's salvific missional purposes are destined to end in frustration.

"Now the Lord said to Abraham, 'Go from your country and your kindred and your father's house to the land that I will show you. And I will make of you a great nation, and I will bless you, and make your name great, so that you will be a blessing...and in you all the families of the earth shall be blessed'" (Gen. 12:1–3).

Abraham's community was to be God's community of blessing to all humankind. Blessing, according to the biblical vision, included infinitely more than mere words of well-wishing. In early Israel, blessing was viewed as the bearer of material and spiritual well-being. God's rule over God's people was a realm of blessedness, the sphere in which the wholeness of God's salvation was experienced in the fruitfulness and the abundance of nature and in social relationships of righteousness and peace. To be a blessing to the nations was to be missional in its truly salvific dimensions.

The call of Abraham to "go from your country and your kindred and your father's house" points to more than a change of geography. It involves knowing and obeying "the Lord, the God of Israel," not the "other gods" of the Chaldeans (Josh. 24:2). As a later Jewish document reports, "This people is descended from the Chaldeans. At one time they lived in Mesopotamia, because they would not follow the gods of their fathers who lived in Chaldea. For they had left the way of their ancestors, and they worshipped the God of heaven, the God they had come to know" (Jth. 5:6–8).

The call of Abraham carried both religious and moral dimensions. To follow the God of Israel called for abandoning Ur, a prime center of agricultural, industrial, commercial, and religious achievements in the ancient world, and its gods, for a life of pilgrimage under the guidance of God. In short, it was a call to radical moral and spiritual nonconformity to Chaldean society and its values. To know the God of Israel was to reorder all of life and all of one's values in accord with God's character. The identity of God's people arises out of God's grace and God's providence. This essentially charismatic character of the people of God is clear from the beginning. This is the point at which the contrast with Babel and its heirs is sharpest. The selfish exercise of power to dominate and to perpetuate domination will always end in confusion of purpose and character. God's people will most faithfully fulfill their calling to serve for the blessing of all the families of the earth precisely when the vision of their missional intention is most focused and their distinctively charismatic identity is sharpest.

The Exodus-Sinai experience in the life of ancient Israel is another moment when God's missional intention for God's people becomes especially clear. "Now therefore, if you will obey my voice and keep my covenant, you shall be my treasured possession out of all the peoples. Indeed, the whole earth is mine, but you shall be for me a priestly kingdom and a holy nation" (Exod. 19:5–6a).

The distinctive character of the children of Abraham kept them from simply being absorbed into Egyptian culture, in spite of their four hundred-year sojourn in Egypt. This "charismatic principle," characteristic of the ancient Hebrews, enabled them to resist assimilation.[5] A people who literally live and survive by the grace of God, and whose character bears the stamp of the God whom they serve will be both missional and counter-cultural, perpetual strangers in society and sojourners with God.

According to the biblical record, Israel's election was based on God's grace and on the fact that they were the least of all peoples (Deut. 7:6-8). This elemental vision of election as God's predilection for the least and the outcasts was deeply rooted in Israel's memory. As ancient Israelites confessed, "A wandering Aramean was my ancestor; he went down into Egypt and lived there as an alien, few in number" (Deut. 26:5). Although Israel later misunderstood this divine election as granting special status and privilege, election is in reality God choosing the weak, the least, and the poor. And this election is to service, to mission. The biblical term translated "possession" in these passages refers to a portion withdrawn from the whole and designated to a special purpose.[6] This puts in context the accompanying phrase, "for all the earth is mine" (Exod. 19:5c).

Israel was chosen as God's special possession, not by its own merits but because of God's saving intention for all nations. Israel's identity hinges on the fact that it is chosen from among all peoples to be a faithful sign of God's salvific intention for all the nations. This calls for a concrete difference. The holiness that characterized Israel should give them no grounds for pride or exclusive claims. It was rather the concrete spiritual and social shape of their vocation. Insofar as Israel was different from the nations,[7] due to its relationship to God, it would be an effective sign of God's saving intention for all humanity. As Israel confessed in its creed, God made them a people from those who had been no people (Deut. 26:5-9; cf. Hos. 2:23). This people of God was called to live in marked contrast to the nations, precisely because its vocation is to be both sign and instrument of salvation for all nations.

The Old Testament prophets kept this vision alive in times of Israel's unfaithfulness and cultural accommodation to the dynamics of

---

[5] Suzanne de Dietrich, *The Witnessing Community: The Biblical Record of God's Purpose* (Philadelphia: Westminster Press, 1958). 46.

[6] Ibid., 54.

[7] This is the sense of the biblical term translated "holy." The original meaning of the root was apparently "separated" or "cut off" from other peoples and practices. P. C. Craigie, *The Book of Deuteronomy* (London: Hodder and Stoughton, 1976), 179.

kingship. While the prophets warned their contemporaries of impending judgment, they also shared a vision of hope beyond judgment, a hope based on the restoration of God's reign of righteousness and peace. Picking up the theme of the ancient promise to Abraham, the prophets perceived the blessing of God's righteous reign reaching to all humanity through the faithful witness of God's restored people. Theirs was a vision of "the mountain of the house of the Lord," established in a new and highly visible way among the peoples of the earth. They envisioned the nations being attracted by the gracious covenant relationships of righteousness, peace, and salvation that characterize God's people (Mic. 4:1–4; cf. Isa. 2:1–4; Zech. 8:20, 22).

Ezekiel, living among the exiles in Babylon, was able to see beyond the narrow nationalism to which some of his contemporaries subscribed. He was able to denounce Israel's unfaithfulness and, at the same time, to envision the nations being blessed by God through the instrumentality of a restored people. "I will sanctify my great name, which has been profaned among the nations, and which you have profaned among them; and the nations shall know that I am the Lord, ...when through you I display my holiness before their eyes" (Ezek. 36:23). And Isaiah, following the return from exile, foresaw the Jewish temple becoming "a house of prayer for all peoples," as well as for the outcasts of Israel and other outsiders (Isa. 56:7–8).

The prophets' hope is that a people who walk in the paths of the Lord, among whom the provisions of God's gracious covenant are concretely realized, will become the magnet that attracts the peoples of the earth. The essential vision of God's holy people becomes the prophetic vision of God's restored people. That vision was anticipated in Abraham's call, a call that required of him absolute dependence on God for both existence and survival. It was also anticipated in the Exodus-Sinai experience, where social relationships were determined by the covenant, and grounded in righteousness and peace.

Jesus, and the messianic movement he initiated, cannot be understood apart from this Old Testament vision of God's missional people. Jesus' kingdom preaching, teaching, and activity all pointed toward the restoration of a holy people commissioned to carry out in a definitive way God's salvific intention in the midst of the nations. The messianic mission was aimed at establishing the eschatological people of God, in which the social order of God's reign would be realized. Jesus perceived the messianic community in terms of the prophetic vision of the "house of the Lord...established as the highest of the mountains." He concretely described this newly restored people of God as "the light of the world, a city built on a hill...that [the peoples] may see your good works and give glory to your Father who is in heaven" (Matt. 5:14–16).

This is the context in which we must understand Jesus' revolutionary calls to the absolute renunciation of violence (Matt. 5:39–48) and coercive domination (Mark 10:42–45) among his followers. The practice of nonresistant love toward violent people and the vision of authority that derives entirely from service imply the existence of a counter-cultural community that stands in sharp contrast to secular societies marked by the will to coerce and to exercise control over others. It is precisely this kind of nonresistant love that witnesses most powerfully to a God who loves his enemies and seeks to save them (Matt. 5:3, 9, 16, 44–48).

In the light of this Old Testament background, the petition in Jesus' prayer, "hallowed be thy name," is an expression of the hope that God will restore a people that is different in its concrete social holiness. It implies the restoration of the true people of God in order that God's reign may shine forth and God's name may stand in all of its glory before all peoples (Ezek. 20:41, 44; 36:22–24; Lev. 20:26; Deut. 7:6–11).[8]

Jesus' teaching on kingdom righteousness (Matthew 5) and confidence in the providence of God (Matt. 6:19–33) also presuppose the kind of community envisioned in the call of Abraham and in God's gracious Sinai covenant, including its sabbatical and jubilee provisions. These teachings all take concrete form in the re-creation of the people of God. In this messianic event, God's reign is being reestablished. A new and different people of God is appearing in the midst of the nations, a people in which God's glory shines forth for the blessing of all peoples (Mic. 4:1–4; Matt. 5:14–16).

If we are to take seriously Mark's description of the event, Jesus literally was crucified because he sought to restore the temple to its function as the house of prayer for all peoples, as envisioned by the prophet Isaiah (Mark 11:17–18; Isa. 56:7). The concrete social form of the messianic community gathered by Jesus was already anticipated in the Old Testament vision of God's counter-cultural people set in the midst of the nations as a sign of God's salvific intention for all. This restored messianic community is the presupposition on which the great commission that Jesus gave is based.

---

[8] Gerhard Lohfink, *Jesus and Community: The Social Dimension of Christian Faith,* trans. John P. Galvin (Philadelphia: Fortress Press, 1984), 14–17, 124.

This is also the vision that inspired the self-understanding of the apostolic communities in the New Testament. They saw themselves as communities of witness to contemporary Judaism and paganism alike. This was the context of their life and mission.

Missional Self-Understanding in 1 Peter

1 Peter 2:9–11 offers a prime example of the way the early church viewed its essential missional identity. "But you are a chosen race, a royal priesthood, a holy nation, God's own people, in order that you may proclaim the mighty acts of him who called you out of darkness into his marvelous light. Once you were not a people, but now you are God's people; once you had not received mercy, but now you have received mercy. Beloved, I urge you as aliens and exiles to abstain from the desires of the flesh that wage war against the soul."

The Old Testament vision of missional peoplehood was vital for the early church's self-understanding. These images of peoplehood were drawn directly from those texts that inspired ancient Israel's sense of identity—Exod. 19:5–6, Deut. 7:6–7, Isa. 43:20–21, and Hos. 1:6–9. The text from 1 Peter explicitly sets forth the missional dimensions of peoplehood.

The appeal in 1 Peter to these Old Testament texts tells us two things about the early church. First, God's saving initiative is essentially corporate in its dimensions. Biblical salvation is relational. It is the restoration of broken relationships—with God, among God's creatures and with all of God's created order. Salvation is experienced in the restoration of all of these relationships. The highly privatized versions of salvation, which modern western Christians have sometimes imagined for themselves, lack solid biblical foundations.

Second, the use of these Old Testament texts shows us that the church considered the character and posture of God's people in the world to be essentially missional. "A royal priesthood" designates a people dedicated to the worship and service of God, their king. It also points to the representative function of a people who exist to bring God's blessing to all peoples, whose calling is to advocacy and to intercession, to life for the benefit of all of God's creatures. The conduct of this people in the midst of the nations must be such that it faithfully, and without distortion, represents the universally saving God whom they have come to know.

"Holy nation" is also an image that points to a people whose identity is determined by the character and salvific purposes of their God.

The context of this image in 1 Peter makes it clear that the holiness envisioned is not first and foremost a matter of individual piety, nor a purely personal or private holiness, important as these may be. The fundamental thrust of this passage is that the people of God as a people give witness to God's salvific intention for all humanity. The unambiguous identity of the early church was a primary ingredient in the fulfillment of its mission. This counter-cultural community is viewed both as the context in which God's mercy is experienced and as the instrument by which that mercy is communicated to the peoples of the earth.

"Chosen race" and "God's own people" are images that reflect the conviction that runs throughout the Old Testament, from Moses to the prophets, and is the basis of Israel's fundamental sense of belonging and purpose. God's people exist for the purpose of blessing all peoples, for effectively communicating God's salvation to all. The Petrine community sensed that, as God's missional people, they were distinctly counter-cultural in their relationship to the world to which they were sent. As a missional people in God's world, they were at home everywhere, but fully at home nowhere. Both Peter and Paul make it clear that peoplehood is an integral part of the good news, as well as an essential instrument in its proclamation. Citing the text from Hos. 1:6–9, Peter states that not to be God's people is to be without mercy; conversely, to be God's people is to experience God's mercy (1 Pet. 2:10). Paul writes that alienation from the commonwealth of Israel is to be "without God in the world" (Eph. 2:12). And conversely, relationship to the Father is found in the context of God's family, in the missional people of God (Eph. 2:18–19).

This vision of missional peoplehood grows out of the vocation of Abraham and the Exodus-Sinai tradition, runs through the prophets, and eventually finds its fullest expression in the New Testament. Jesus himself fulfilled this understanding of peoplehood and mission (Matt. 5:13–16, et al.) and both Peter and Paul, as well as other New Testament writers, articulated it for the early church.

MISSIONAL PEOPLEHOOD IN THE EARLY CHURCH

The vision of God's saving predilection for the weak, the least, and the outsiders was an essential ingredient in Israel's sense of identity. It was deeply rooted in the vocation of Abraham and the Exodus-Sinai experience and freely owned in Israel's ancient creed (Deut. 26:5–9). But this vision of God's saving activity in favor of the widow, the orphan, and the stranger, reflected in the prophets, reaches its biblical climax in Jesus' own mission. Jesus revealed a God who seeks and saves the outsiders—tax collectors, sinners, the ceremonially unclean, lepers, Galileans, Samaritans and pagans, women (including those of ill repute), and children. Jesus' ragtag group of followers, who were later consolidated into that missional community of the Spirit we see following Pentecost, was a prime example of his compassion for outsiders. And, as we have seen, this led to the animosity of Jewish authorities and eventually to his crucifixion.

To its enormous credit, the primitive church kept this vision intact. The early church understood itself as a counter-cultural missional community of God's kingdom. The church assumed the same vision of God's kingship that had inspired Jesus in his messianic mission of kingdom restoration. "[God] executes justice for the oppressed; ...gives food to the hungry. The LORD sets the prisoners free; the LORD opens the eyes of the blind. The LORD lifts up those who are bowed down, the LORD loves the righteous. The LORD watches over the strangers; he upholds the orphan and the widow" (Ps. 146:7–9). The fulfillment of God's salvific intention for all peoples is this missional community's reason for being.

The Jew-Gentile debate in the Acts of the Apostles can be best understood, I think, in this perspective. Pagan outsiders figure prominently, even in the Gospel of Matthew, the most "Jewish" of the Gospels. Women of ill repute and of pagan origin are featured in the genealogy of Jesus. Women are the first witnesses to the resurrection. From the lips of a hated imperial agent, we hear that Jesus is truly the Son of God. Political prisoners were among the primary writers of the New Testament documents.

This is the vision and practice of the early church that spilled over into the second century. Women were protagonists in the life of the early church to a degree unequaled in contemporary Judaism or among their pagan neighbors. In fact, women are thought to have been among the church's most effective evangelizers during the first two centuries, as the church spread throughout the empire. While systematic thought about mission, encouragement to evangelize, prayer for the conversion of pagans, and even the existence of formal missionaries were almost absent from early Christian writings, Christian communities were

The Church: Missional Community of the Kingdom 133

intentionally missional.[9] The "women's house," the central courtyard, in which family life and work were centered and community interaction took place, was a primary place where authentic evangelization happened.

Christians of Jewish origin overcame their ancient ethnic prejudices and hatred of Samaritans and pagans, sharing their tables, their homes, and their unbounded love with those who had been deemed their enemies. As Justin Martyr tells it, where the logic of debate failed to convince, the depth and quality of the love with which these Christians related to one another, and even to their enemies, and the personal abandonment with which they fearlessly faced death, were highly persuasive.[10] Even threats of death could not diminish their loyalty or silence their fearless witness to the One whom they confessed to be their Lord in a kingdom they proclaimed to be not of this world.

They persuaded their detractors not by force of logic or eloquence but by the quality of their lives, so that even unlettered old women in their midst became apologists for the cause of the kingdom. Runaway slaves, hiding in the great cities of the Roman Empire, found new life and hope as they were incorporated freely as equals into early Christian communities. One of these ex-slaves, Hermas, became an outstanding leader of the church in Rome early in the second century. His writings were at one point even considered for inclusion in the primitive Christian canon. Rather than abandoning unwanted children, as their pagan contemporaries were accustomed to doing, Christians regularly made the rounds of the city dumps, rescuing discarded babies and raising them as their own. These modest house churches were in fact missional communities characterized by loving compassion.

The similarities between the early church and the primitive Sacramentarian and Anabaptist movements in the Low Countries are remarkable. These also became popular movements, missional in character. From their beginning they too showed a compassion that attracted the marginalized sectors of society. These included peasants and artisans, laborers and fisherfolk, the poor and the unlettered, women, and others who found themselves on the fringes of society. They

---

[9] Alan Kreider, "Worship and Evangelism in Pre-Christendom (The Laing Lecture 1994)," *Vox Evangelica* 24 (1994): 8.

[10] Justin Martyr *Apology* 2.12–13; in Alexander Roberts and James Donaldson, eds., *The Apostolic Fathers with Justin Martyr and Irenaeus,* vol. 1 of *The Ante-Nicene Fathers* (New York: Charles Scribner's Sons, 1925), 192–93.

effectively broke the sacramental and ecclesiastical monopoly that an ecclesio-clerical elite held over the means of grace, and in the process transformed their understanding of the church—a missional community in which all participate fully.

The glory of the early Sacramentarian and Anabaptist movements was not so much in their heroic ability to remain morally "stain resistant" or "wrinkle free," as some in the movement later hoped. It was rather in their daring counter-cultural openness to outsiders, risking death itself in order to open the means of grace to the marginalized. Menno was surely representative of the movement in gladly accepting the ignominy that solidarity with outcasts and heretics brought. He vigorously defended the poor and the have-nots against the calumnies and slanderous charges of the rich and the powerful.[11]

The secret of their vitality lies, I think, in their capacity to envision the church not so much in terms of status as in dynamic missional terms. Anabaptists not only defined the church minimally in terms of its perceived essence (teaching the Word, observing the sacraments), but also in missional terms. Menno, as we have seen, included obedience to God's Word manifested in holiness of life; sincere and unfeigned love for others; faithful confession of Christ's name, will, Word, and ordinance "in the face of all cruelty, tyranny, tumult, fire, sword, and violence of the world"; and the cross of Christ borne by all his disciples for the sake of his testimony and Word.[12] I have a feeling that what gave the Anabaptist movement in the Low Countries its vigor and vitality and made it so attractive to the marginalized social classes was its insistence on the missional character of the church as compassionate community of God's kingdom. I doubt that a focus on its ontological and institutional character would have had the same appeal for people who felt left out by the religious institutions of the period.

CONCLUSION

We Mennonites in North America stand at a crucial point in our history. We can, like Christendom, understand ourselves ontologically and somewhat statically, in terms of what we perceive our essential nature to be. We can try to agree on our boundaries in order to define clearly who we are and what we are about, who is in and who is not. This stance is

---

[11] *The Complete Writings of Menno Simons*, 307, 558, 674, et al.

[12] Ibid., 739–41.

probably characterized by an underlying concern for conserving the purity of the church.

On the other hand, we can seek to envision a new Mennonite church in dynamic and missional terms. Here the overriding concern of the church will not focus so much on its essence or being as on its desire to see the saving purposes of God's kingdom fulfilled for the salvation of all. Here the concern will not be so much for "holding the line" against perceived dangers threatening the life of the church as for putting our lives on the line for the cause of Christ and his kingdom.

Our review of the story of God's people, both biblical and postbiblical, has reminded us of God's overriding concern for the restoration of all creation. This helps to explain the divine predilection for the broken, the weak, the suffering, the sick, the little ones, the outcasts, the poor, the oppressed, the marginalized, the outsiders, the lost. As we read in the Gospels, this was Jesus concern, too. In both deed and word, Jesus communicated the overwhelming love of a compassionate God who cares and who saves. The Gospels also show us that the invitation to follow Jesus is an invitation to participate with him in God's salvific mission in the world. In fact the fundamental shape of the church's mission must be determined by Jesus' own mission (Matt. 9:35–10:42).

Among other things, this means that we may be less concerned about securing our own ecclesiastical future because we are confident that the future is secure in God's hands. After all, from the perspective of God's reign over restored creation, the church is expendable. This means that the church may safely shift its principal attention from its own future and its own maintenance, and assume the risks of unconditional love and compassion toward all who are the objects of God's compassion and loving concern. Rather than focusing our human and material resources on our congregations and institutions, we could be freed to expend them at the periphery. From the biblical record, it seems that vulnerability is the only posture from which an authentically saving gospel can be communicated.

Questions about the institutional forms of integration, authority, polity, accountability, both intra- and inter-congregational, will continue to concern us. But they should not become the objects of our ultimate concern. When we shift our focus from a predominately ontological vision of the church to a missional perspective, our attention tends to move away from ourselves and our own well-being to God's concern— the restoration of broken creation (including humanity) to the shalom God originally intended for all God's creatures.

I am convinced that the gospel dictum, repeated by the evangelists, is true in its corporate sense as well as in a personal one. "Those who want to save their life will lose it, and those who lose their life for my sake, and for the sake of the gospel, will save it" (Mark 8:35; cf. Matt. 10:39; 16:25; Luke 9:24; John 12:25). This also applies to the church. According to the gospel, herein lies the secret for communicating authentic life in God's kingdom. It also encloses the secret of the church's future in God's ongoing purposes.

Contributors

Lois Barrett
Executive Secretary, General Conference Commission on Home Ministries, Newton, Kansas

Jo-Ann Brant
Professor of Bible and Religion, Goshen College, Goshen, Indiana

John Driver
Missionary (retired), Mennonite Board of Missions, Elkhart, Indiana

Jacob W. Elias
Professor of New Testament, Associated Mennonite Biblical Seminary, Elkhart, Indiana

James Juhnke
Professor of History, Bethel College, North Newton, Kansas

Karl Koop
Associate Director, Institute of Mennonite Studies; Assistant Professor of Anabaptist-Mennonite Studies, Associated Mennonite Biblical Seminary, Elkhart, Indiana

J. Nelson Kraybill
President, Associated Mennonite Biblical Seminary, Elkhart, Indiana

Ben C. Ollenburger
Professor of Biblical Theology, Associated Mennonite Biblical Seminary, Elkhart, Indiana

A. James Reimer
Professor of Religion and Theology, Conrad Grebel College, Waterloo, Ontario, and Toronto School of Theology, Toronto, Ontario

John D. Roth
Professor of History, Goshen College, Goshen, Indiana

Mary Schertz
Director, Institute of Mennonite Studies; Professor of New Testament, Associated Mennonite Biblical Seminary, Elkhart, Indiana

www.ingramcontent.com/pod-product-compliance
Lightning Source LLC
Chambersburg PA
CBHW072155160426
43197CB00012B/2389